WIRE
JEWELRY

in an afternoon®

WIRE JEWELRY

in an afternoon®

MICKEY BASKETT

Sterling Publishing Co., Inc.
New York

Prolific Impressions Production Staff:

Editor: Mickey Baskett
Creative Design: Susan E. Mickey
Copy: Sylvia Carroll
Graphics: Lampe•Farley Communications
Photography: Jerry Mucklow
Styling: Kirsten Werner Jones
Administration: Jim Baskett

Library of Congress Cataloging-in-Publication Data Available

10 9 8 7 6 5 4 3 2 1

First paperback edition published in 2002 by
Sterling Publishing Company, Inc.
387 Park Avenue South, New York, N.Y. 10016
Produced by Prolific Impressions, Inc.
160 South Candler St., Decatur, GA 30030
©2001 by Prolific Impressions, Inc.
Distributed in Canada by Sterling Publishing
c/o Canadian Manda Group, One Atlantic Avenue, Suite 105
Toronto, Ontario, Canada M6K 3E7
Distributed in Australia by Capricorn Link (Australia) Pty. Ltd.
P.O. Box 704, Windsor, NSW 2756 Australia

Printed in China

Sterling ISBN 0-8069-2969-3 Hardcover
        ISBN 0-4027-0132-2 Paperback

Acknowledgments

Mickey Baskett thanks the following people for their generous contributions:

The artists who contributed their talent to this book. These individuals have been generous enough to share their talent and knowledge of designing with wire. The following designers made this book possible: **Patty Cox, Diana Thomas, Caren Carr,** and **Pat McMahon**.

For Wire Supplies:
• Nasco Arts and Crafts, 901 Janesville Avenue, P.O. Box 901, Fort Atkinson, WI; Phone 920-563-2446
• Artistic Wire, Elmhurst, IL, www.artisticwire.com

WIRE JEWELRY • *In an Afternoon*

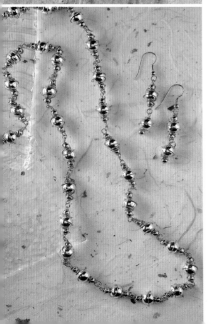

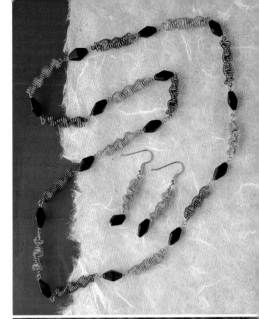

*I*f you have ever looked at jewelry in a department store or a clothing boutique and mumbled to your friend, "I could make that," this book is for you! Wire jewelry can be easy and fun ... especially with these simple projects. With readily available supplies and easy to use instructions, you will spend a delightful afternoon or evening with beautiful results to wear and enjoy.

These projects have been geared specifically for the busy person with an eye for creativity and more ideas than time. Using just a few basic tools, you can bend, twist, and wrap your way to dazzling distinctive jewelry. Step-by-step instructions, numerous illustrations, and complete patterns are provided.

In the project photos you can see the vast array of colors and textures achieved with wire. The designs are varied and unique, for every taste and style. There are cute kicky projects for young teens and classic styles for sophisticated adults. The adaptability of wire to many techniques will inspire you to create and embellish with your own personal flair.

The best thing about these inexpensive and easy to make accessories will be the compliments and comments from your friends. You will beam with pride and satisfaction as you say, "I made it myself."

All About Wire

Wire is the generic name given to pliable metallic strands that are made in a variety of thicknesses and lengths. Two basic characteristics distinguish one kind of wire from another: the type of metal used and the thickness, usually referred to as the gauge or diameter. The higher the number of the gauge, the thinner the wire; e.g., 24 gauge wire is thinner than 16 gauge wire. The "supplies" lists of the projects in this book list the type of metal and the thickness used.

The type of metal a wire is made of gives the wire its color. Wire is often referred to by the names of three metallic "colors"—gold, silver, and copper. **Gold-colored wire** can be made of gold, brass, or bronze. **Silver-colored wire** can be made of silver, steel, aluminum, or tin-coated copper. **Copper-colored wire** is made of copper or copper plus another metal. The color of wire can be altered with spray paint, acrylic craft paint, or rub-on metallic wax. Wire can also be purchased in colors.

Commercially, wire is used to impart structure and conduct electricity, so it's not surprising that it is sold in hardware and building supply stores and electrical supply houses.

You'll also find wire for sale in art supply stores, in craft stores, in stores that sell supplies for jewelry making, and from mail order catalogs.

Types of Wire Used in Projects

Most any type of wire will work for the projects in this book. Just be sure to use the thickness of wire listed in the supplies list to get the same result as shown. It is best to use a wire that is noncorrosive so your projects will have a long life. All of the wire types listed are very pliable and easy to work with.

Wire can be found at a variety of places. Hardware stores carry an infinite number of wire types. However, sometimes the wire from hardware stores is not coated and may rust. Beading shops and craft shops is a good source for the type of wire you will need for making jewelry. There are also a number of websites for jewelry crafting that carry a wide range of wire types and sizes.

Use any of the following wire types for the projects in this book:

Thin gauge wire or beading wire: Sold by the spool or the package, thinner wire—from 16 to 28 gauge—can be made of a variety of metals, including sterling silver, brass, gold, copper, steel, and galvanized tin. You can find it in hobby shops, craft stores, hardware stores, and stores that sell supplies for jewelry making.

Armature wire: A non-corrosive aluminum alloy wire, armature wire is easy to bend and doesn't tarnish. It is used by clay sculptors to build their armatures—the wire framework sculptures are built on. It is usually 1/8" or 1/4" thick or can be found by gauge measurement. You'll find it in stores that sell art and craft supplies.

Buss wire: Buss wire is tin-coated copper wire used as an uninsulated conductor of electricity. Shinier than aluminum wire and inexpensive, buss wire is silver in color and often used for making jewelry. It is available in various gauges. Look for it at hardware stores and electrical supply houses.

Aluminum Wire: Soft and flexible, aluminum wire is silver in color and has a dull finish. It won't rust and is often available at building supply and hardware stores.

Solder wire: Used by plumbers to solder pipe, solder wire is soft, silver-colored, and easy to bend. It comes on a spool and is sold by the pound. Be sure to buy solder that is solid core and lead-free. It can be found at hardware and building supply stores.

Wire mesh: This is becoming a popular material for crafting. It can be found at craft shops or beading shops in small rolls about 4"-5" wide. It can be found also in hardware stores — and is used for window screens and filters and also called "wire cloth." Wire mesh is available in brass, bronze, copper, and the more common aluminum. At hardware stores, it can be found on rolls that are 36" wide and is sold by the foot. The number of the mesh (40 mesh, 100 mesh) denotes the number of holes per inch. Wire mesh with higher numbers is finer—almost like fabric—and is made of thinner wire.◖

Pictured clockwise from top right: 1/4" armature wire; 1/8" armature wire, 19 gauge wire, 24 gauge galvanized wire, 16 gauge brass wire, solder wire, #40 wire mesh.

Colored wire on spools especially marketed for jewelry making and crafting.

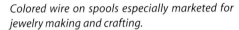

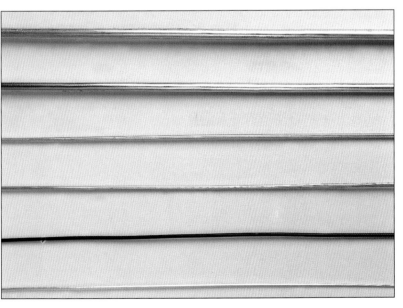

Various wires used are shown actual size on left. From top to bottom: 1/8" armature wire, 16 oz. solder wire, 16 gauge buss wire, 16 gauge brass wire, 19 gauge black wire, 24 gauge galvanized wire.

Tools and Equipment

Pliers

Pliers are used for bending, twisting, looping, and coiling wire.

Jewelry making pliers are the best type to use when working with delicate projects and materials.

Round nose pliers have rounded ends. Use smaller ones for delicate work and larger ones to make bigger loops.

Needlenose pliers or flat nose pliers, also called "snipe nose pliers," have flat inner surfaces and pointed ends.

Nylon jaw pliers will prevent scratching of metal surfaces.

Cutters

Available in a wide range of sizes, **wire cutters** are tools used for cutting wire. Thicker, lower gauge wire requires sturdy cutters. Very thin wire can be cut with smaller jewelry-making wire cutters. Very thin wire can be cut with **scissors** or **nail clippers** but it will dull these tools. Use **old scissors** or **metal shears** for cutting wire mesh.

Often pliers have a sharp edge that can be used for cutting wire. Use a **small file** for smoothing cut edges of wire or any rough spots.

Supplies for Making Templates

For some projects, instructions are given for creating templates from wood and dowels or nails for forming the wire. These are also called "jigs." To make a template, you will need:

Tracing paper for tracing the pattern for the template.

Transfer paper and a stylus for transferring the pattern.

Piece of wood for the template surface

Small headless nails (3/4" wire brads work well in most cases) of small diameter

Dowels for forming the wire. If you make a template using dowels, you'll also need a drill with a drill bit to make the holes for the dowels.

A jig with pegs can also be purchased ready-made.

Glues

Several types of glue are used in wire projects. When using glue, be cautious! Many glues emit fumes as they dry. Always read the label and follow manufacturer's precautions and instructions. Work in a ventilated area and avoid contact with your skin.

Jewelry glue is a clear-drying glue made specifically for gluing metal and stones. Find it at craft stores and stores that sell jewelry-making supplies.

Metal glue is just that—a glue that is meant to adhere metal to metal. Find it at crafts and hardware stores.

Household cement is a general purpose cement sold under a variety of trade names. It can be used for metal, china, glass, and paper. It is available at crafts and hardware stores.

Epoxy comes in two containers—one contains a resin, the other a hardener. When mixed, their chemical interaction creates a strong, clear bond. You'll find epoxy at crafts and hardware stores.

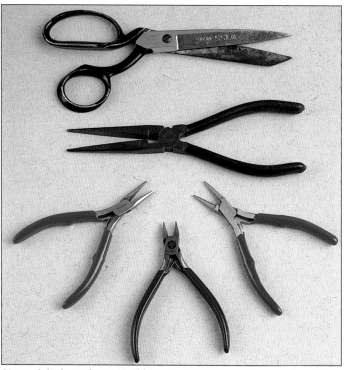

Pictured clockwise from top: old scissors, needlenose pliers, round nose jewelry pliers, wire cutters, flat nose jewelry pliers.

Beads and Stones

Beads are made all over the world and can be found at crafts stores and the notions departments of variety and department stores. There are literally hundreds of shapes, sizes, and colors from which to choose. Beads are made of a variety of materials, including glass, wood, ceramics, metal, acrylic, semi-precious stones, and natural minerals. They are classified according to material, shape, and size. Beads have holes in them for stringing or threading on wire.

Stones don't have holes for stringing or threading, so when used with wire, they are wrapped with wire or glued in place. They may be of glass, natural minerals, acrylic, or semi- precious stones.

Cabochons are stones that are flat on one side, making them ideal for decorating flat surfaces.

Jewelry Findings

Findings are the metal items that transform wire and beads into jewelry. You will need the following:

Clasps: These come in a wide variety of shapes, sizes, and designs. Choose the type you like best. You will find barrel clasps, spring lock clasps, and fish hook/box clasps.

Pictured clockwise from top right: natural bone beads, metal beads, glass cabochons, glass beads—frosted and clear.

Jump rings are small metal rings that are used to attach one finding to another such as attaching an eyepin to an earring back. They are split so that they can be pried open and shut for use.

Earring backs come in both pierced and unpierced varieties. Pierced backs fall into two categories: *hooks* and *posts*. Unpierced backs are available in screw-on and *clip-on* styles.

Stickpins and pin backs are attached to your jewelry design to transform it into a pin.

Headpins are earring findings used to construct drop earrings. They come in a variety of lengths. Beads are threaded onto the pin, then attached to an earring back. The headpin looks like a straight pin without a point at the tip.

Eyepins have a loop on the end and are used in the same manner as headpins. A jump ring can be attached through the eye of the pin when needed.

Protective Gear

Wire can be sharp at the ends and could cause injury if caution is not used. For safety, wear **goggles** when nipping wire and **protective gloves** such as cotton or leather gardening gloves.❁

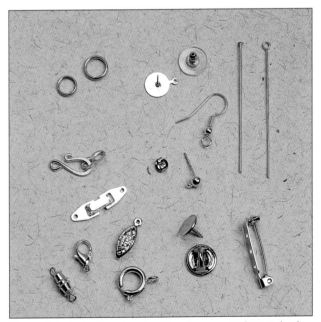

Pictured clockwise from top right: headpin, eyepin, bar pin back, push pin back, various clasps, two sizes of jump rings, pierced earring posts and backs.

General Instructions

The following techniques are used in some, not all, of the projects.
Most of the projects merely require that you bend and shape the wire.

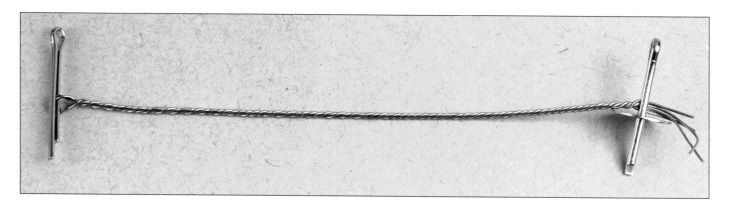

Making a Perfectly Symmetrical Twist

You Will Need

2 cotter pins, 2" x 3/16"
1 fender washer, 1-1/4" x 3/16"
2 pieces 16 gauge wire, each 24" long

Follow These Steps

1. Thread the wires through the eye of one cotter pin and fold wires in half at center around cotter pin. *(Fig. 1)*
2. Slide the cut ends between the arms of a second cotter pin. Hold ends of wires flat in cotter pin. Tighten the hold by sliding a fender washer on the end of the second cotter pin. *(Fig. 1)*
3. Slide folded ends down between arms of first cotter pin. *(Fig. 2)*
4. Holding a cotter pin in each hand, twist one pin toward you while twisting the other pin away from you to make a rope-like strand. *(Fig. 2)*
5. Remove pins from twisted wire.❮

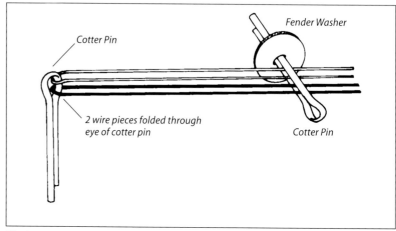

Cotter Pin

Fender Washer

2 wire pieces folded through eye of cotter pin

Cotter Pin

Fig. 1

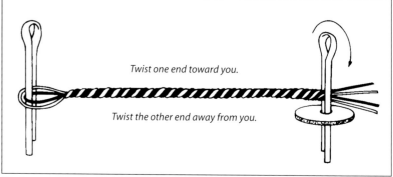

Twist one end toward you.

Twist the other end away from you.

Fig. 2

How To Coil Wire with a Drill

You Will Need
Supplies:
Buss wire, 16 gauge: 10" length
Higher gauge spool wire

Tools:
Power drill

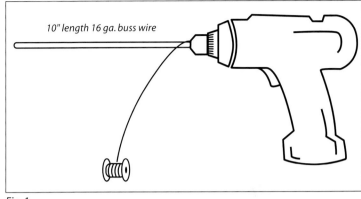

10" length 16 ga. buss wire

Fig. 1

Follow These Steps
1. Insert a 10" piece of buss wire and the end of the higher gauge spool wire into drill. Allow spool of higher gauge wire to drop. Close and secure wire ends in drill. *(Fig. 1)*
2. Set drill speed to slow. Slowly run drill and pinch wires, allowing spool wire to coil around buss wire. Compress coiled wire tightly against drill. Continue coiling the wire to length of coiled wire desired. Remove coil from buss wire. *(Fig. 2)*

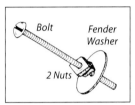

Fig. 2

Constructing a Flat Coil Maker

You Will Need:
1 threaded bolt, 2" x 3/16"
3 nuts, 3/16"
2 fender washers, 1-1/4" x 3/16"
16 gauge wire
File
Needlenose pliers

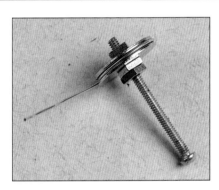

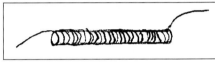

Bolt   Fender Washer

2 Nuts

Fig. 1

Notch

Fig. 2

Follow These Steps
1. Screw two nuts on the bolt about 3/4" from threaded end. Add one fender washer. *(Fig. 1)*
2. File a small notch on inside opening of other fender washer. *(Fig. 2)*
3. Make a 30 degree bend in wire 3/16" from the end. *(Fig. 3)*
4. Hook bend of wire in notch of fender washer. *(Fig. 4)*
5. Slide notched fender washer on bolt next to first fender washer, with the wire length between the washers. The bent tip of the wire should be on outside of washers. Screw remaining nut

tightly against second washer. *(Fig. 5)*
6. Hold stem of bolt in fingers of one hand with thumb on top of fender washer near the threaded end. Hold length of wire in other hand. Turn bolt to form a flat coil of wire between the washers. Press top of washer with thumb while turning to open coiling side of washers. *(Fig. 6)*
7. When wire coil reaches desired size or the edge of the washer, unscrew bolt from end. Remove washer and coil from bolt.
8. Trim starting bend in wire with cutting edge of needlenose pliers.❆

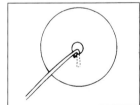

Fig. 3

Fig. 4

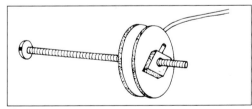

Fig. 5

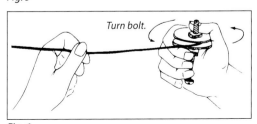

Turn bolt.

Fig. 6

Wrapped Wire Jewelry

These projects all involve wrapping wire around a bead or a shape. This is an easy and beautiful way to create something out of the ordinary. Look at these wrapped beads and let your imagination roam. These projects all use fine wire and simple tools. Wrap yourself in these wire jewels.

Wrapped Silver and Gold
Necklace and Earrings

Designed by Patty Cox

Finished Length of Necklace: 28"
Finished Length of Earring (excluding finding): 1-1/2"

You Will Need

Supplies:
Gold wire, 24 gauge
Silver beads, 8mm
Gold beads, 4mm
Jump rings, 1/8"
Necklace clasp
Set of fish hook earring findings

Tools:
Round nose pliers
Needlenose pliers

Follow These Steps

Wrap the Beads:
1. Cut a 12" length of gold wire. Hold the wire 1/2" from the end of the round nose pliers. Fold the wire over the round nose pliers to form a loop. (Fig. 1).
2. Add a 4mm gold bead, an 8mm silver bead, and another 4mm gold bead over both wires. Form a wire loop on the other end of the beads. Wrap wire tightly around loop. (Fig. 2)

3. Spiral wire around all three beads. End wire tightly around other loop. (Fig. 3) Clip wire ending tail as needed. Repeat for each group of beads. Make 36 bead groups—32 for necklace and two for each earring.

Assemble the Necklace:
1. Connect 33 bead groups with jump rings.
2. Attach necklace clasp pieces to ends.

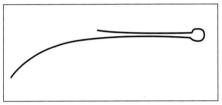

Fig. 1

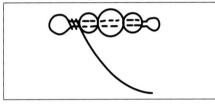

Fig. 2

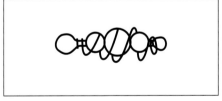

Fig. 3

Assemble the Earrings:
1. Connect two bead groups for each earring.
2. Add a jump ring to one end of each group (will be the top).
3. Attach bead dangles to fish hook earwires by connecting jump rings to earwires. (Fig. 4) ☾

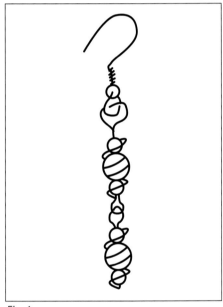

Fig. 4

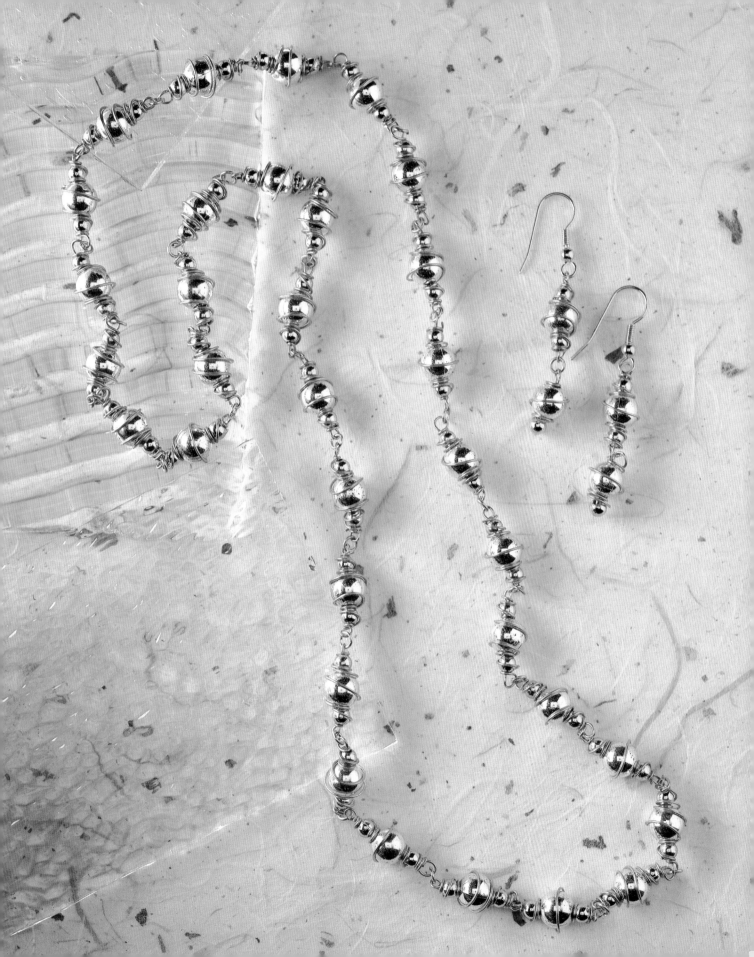

Wrapped Bugle Beads & Seeds
Necklace and Earrings

Designed by Patty Cox

Finished Length of Necklace: 21"
Finished Length of Earring (excluding finding): 2"

You Will Need

Supplies:
Gold wire, 28 gauge
Purple-blue glass seed beads
Purple-blue glass round beads, 2mm
Gold round beads, 4mm
Turquoise bugle beads, 5/8" long
Two cobalt round beads, 6mm
Jump rings, 1/8"
Four 2" gold eyepins
Set of fish hook earring findings

Tools:
Round nose pliers
Needlenose pliers

Follow These Steps

Wrap the bugle Beads:
1. Cut an 8" length of gold wire. Hold wire at 1/2" from end with round nose pliers. Fold wire over round nose to form a loop. *(Fig. 1)*
2. Add a bugle bead over both wires. *(Fig. 2)* Form a wire loop on other end of bead. Wrap wire tightly around loop. *(Fig. 3)*
3. Add a 1" strand of seed beads onto wire. *(Fig. 4)* Spiral beaded wire around bugle bead. *(Fig. 5)*. End wire tightly around other loop. Clip wire ending tail as needed.
4. Repeat steps 1-3 for 14 bugle bead units.

Wrap Round Beads:
1. Cut a 4" length of gold wire. Hold it at 1/2" from end with round nose pliers and make a loop as you did for bugle beads. *(Fig. 1)*
2. Add a 2mm purple-blue bead, a 4mm gold bead, and another 2mm purple-blue bead over both wires.*(Fig. 6)* Form a wire loop on other end of beads. Wrap wire tightly around loop. Clip ending tail as needed.

3. Repeat steps 1 and 2 for 13 groups.

Assemble the Necklace:
1. Alternate bugle bead units and round bead units, connecting them with jump rings.
2. Connect necklace ends to a clasp

Assemble the Earrings: *(See Fig. 7)*
1. Wrap a 5/8" turquoise bugle bead with seed beads.
2. Insert the following onto an eyepin: 4mm gold bead, 6mm cobalt bead, 4mm gold bead, wrapped bugle. Form top end of eyepin into a loop, using round nose pliers.
3. For lower dangle, insert onto an eyepin: 2mm purple-blue bead, 4mm gold bead, 2mm purple- blue bead. Form remaining wire end into a coil, using round nose pliers.
4. Connect the two dangles with a jump ring. Hang bugle end of earring onto a fish hook earwire.
5. Repeat steps 1-4 for other earring.

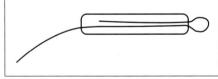

Fig. 1

Fig. 2

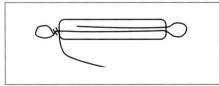

Fig. 3

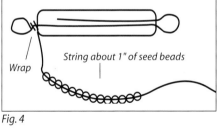

Wrap

String about 1" of seed beads

Fig. 4

Fig. 5

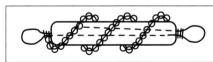

Wrap wire tightly

Fig. 6

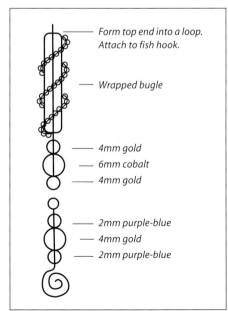

Form top end into a loop. Attach to fish hook.

Wrapped bugle

4mm gold
6mm cobalt
4mm gold

2mm purple-blue
4mm gold
2mm purple-blue

Fig. 7 — Earring

Wrapped Bugle Beads
Necklace

Designed by Patty Cox

Finished Length of Necklace: 29-1/2"

You Will Need

Supplies:
Gold wire, 24 gauge
Cobalt blue glass beads, 4mm
Cobalt blue bugle beads, 1" long
Turquoise bugle beads, 5/8" long
Jump rings, 1/8"
Necklace clasp

Tools:
Round nose pliers
Needlenose pliers

Follow These Steps

Wrap the Bugle Beads:
1. Cut a 6" length of gold wire. Holding wire 1/2" from end with round nose pliers, fold wire over round nose to form a loop. *(Fig. 1)*
2. Add a bugle bead over both wires. *(Fig. 2)* Form a wire loop on the other end of bead. Wrap wire tightly around loop, then continue spiraling wire around the bugle bead. *(Fig. 3)* Wrap wire tightly around other loop. Clip wire end as needed.
3. Repeat steps 1 and 2 for all bugle beads. Make 22 bugle bead units—14 turquoise and eight cobalt blue.

Cobalt Beads:
1. Cut a 4" length of gold wire. Holding wire 1/2" from end with round nose pliers, fold wire over round nose to form a loop. *(Fig. 1)*
2. Add a cobalt bead over both wires. Form a wire loop on other end of bead Wrap wire tightly around loop. *(Fig. 4)* Clip wire end as needed.
3. Repeat steps 1 and 2 to all cobalt beads. Make 7 cobalt bead units.

Assemble the Necklace:
1. Attach beads with jump rings in this order: cobalt bugle, turquoise bugle, cobalt round, turquoise bugle, repeat sequence until bead units are all used.
2. Attach necklace ends to a necklace clasp with jump rings. *(Fig. 5)*

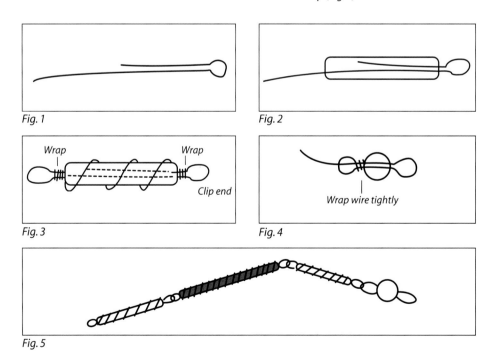

Fig. 1

Fig. 2

Fig. 3

Fig. 4

Fig. 5

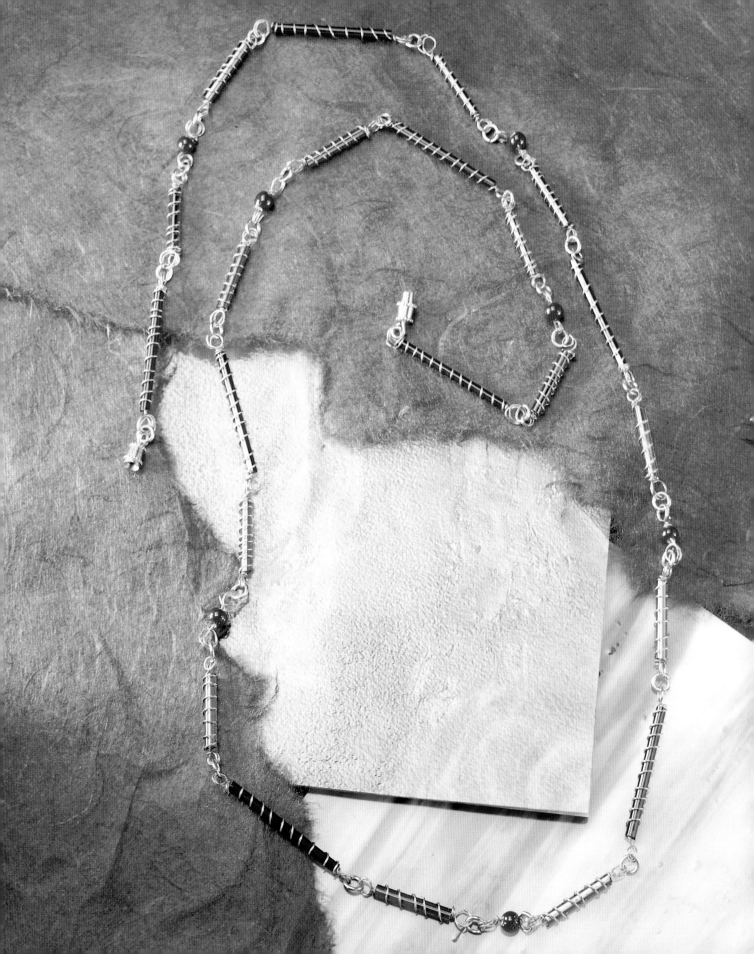

Wrapped Bead ID Holder
ID Chain and Earrings

Designed by Patty Cox

Finished Length of Necklace: 30"
Finished Length of Earring (excluding finding): 2-1/2"

You Will Need
Supplies:
Gold wire, 24 gauge
Gold wire, 20 gauge
Assorted glass beads, various sizes from 4mm to 20mm
Gold beads, 4mm
4mm gold Indian bells, 2 for earrings
Jump rings, 1/8"
Fingernail clipped earring finding (normally used as a clip earring finding for pierced ears)
Set of fish hook earring findings

Tools:
Round nose pliers
Needlenose pliers

Follow These Steps
Wrap the Beads:
1. Cut a 12" length of 24 gauge gold wire. Hold wire at 1" from end with round nose pliers and fold wire in half over round nose to form a loop. *(Fig. 1)*
2. Add a 4mm gold bead over both wires, then a glass bead of any size and color, and another 4mm gold bead. Form a loop on other end of beads. Wrap wire tightly around loop.
3. Continue spiraling wire around beads. End wire tightly around other loop. *(Fig. 2)*. Clip wire end as needed.
4. Repeat steps 1 thru 3 for 24 bead units. *Note: the length of the necklace will be determined by the size of the glass beads used.*
5. Make some 3-bead units with a 4mm gold bead, a small glass bead (4-6mm) and a 4mm gold bead. Make these the same as above, but do not spiral the wire around

the glass beads. I used around 6 of these units in necklace.

Make a Wrapped Wire Spiral:
1. Cut a 16" length of 20 gauge gold wire. Fold wire end back 3/4" over round nose pliers, forming a loop. *(Fig. 3)* Grasp wire 1" from loop with round nose pliers and form another loop. *(Fig. 4)*
2. Tightly wrap the wire shaft between loops with the wire end. *(Fig. 5)*
3. Loosely wrap the wire in a spiral around shaft, adding a bead on the spiral. *(Fig. 6)*
4. Wrap end tightly at loop. *(Fig. 7)*

Assemble the Necklace:
1. Attach bead units together with jump rings. Attach ends with a jump ring.
2. To form a strand of drop beads, attach three beads with jump rings. Wire the fingernail clip jewelry finding to end of bead strand. *(Fig. 8)*

3. Attach drop strand to necklace with a jump ring. *(Fig. 9)*

Assemble the Earrings:
1. Make three wrapped bead units and one wrapped wire spiral as instructed previously.
2. Attach two units together with a jump ring for each earring.
3. Attach one Indian bell on one end of each earring.
4. Attach to fish hook earwire with a jump ring to the other end of each earring.⟨

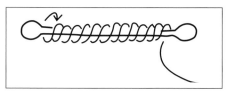
Fig. 5

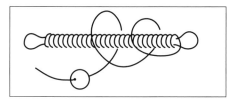
Fig. 6

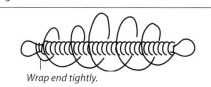
Wrap end tightly.
Fig. 7

Fig. 1

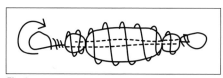
Fig. 2

Fig. 3

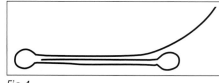
Fig. 4

Fingernail clip earring finding
Fig. 8

Fig. 9

daisy
daycare

DOB: 03-15-69
HT: 5-10
EYES: BLU

Sally Smith
101 Maple Dr.
Hometown TX 78900

Sally Smith

Spirals & Coils Jewelry

Spirals and coils and twists of all kinds add much interest to wire jewelry. These shapes are abundant in nature and are, as such, very appealing to the human aesthetic sense.

You probably wouldn't guess the number of variations on these themes. There are flat spirals. There are three-dimensional coils. There are three dimensional coils twisted into three dimensional spirals. There are tight spirals and coils, and loose, rather open ones. Large wire makes contemporary looking spirals, while thin wire makes dainty spirals and fine coils.

See how many more ways you can think of to spiral and coil your way to beauty.

Copper Spiral Twist
Necklace and Earrings

Designed by Patty Cox

Finished Length of Necklace: 28"
Finished Length of Earring (excluding finding): 1-3/4"

You Will Need

Supplies:
Copper wire, 22 gauge
Antique copper (brown) wire, 22 gauge
Diamond shaped matte black beads
Jump rings, 1/8"
Two gold eyepins
Set of fish hook earring findings

Tools:
Mini craft stick
Round nose pliers
Needlenose pliers

Follow These Steps

Form the Spiral Beads:

1. Mark two lines 3/4" apart on a mini craft stick. *(Fig. 1)*
2. Place a 3" tail of the wire along the edge of the craft stick. Wrap wire over tail and around craft stick between marks. Compress wraps tightly and wrap as many times as possible without overlapping between the marks. *(Fig. 2)*
3. Trim the 3" wire tail extending beyond the wraps to approximately 3/8". Form it into a loop, using round nose pliers. *(Fig. 3)*
4. Remove wire from craft stick. Using needlenose pliers, twist a loop in the first wire wrap. *(Fig. 4)*
5. Gently twist wire into a spiral with your fingers. *(Fig. 5)*
6. Follow steps 2-5 to make nine spirals with copper wire (seven for necklace and one for each earring) and seven spirals with antique copper wire (all for necklace).

Diamond Beads:

1. Cut a 6" length of copper wire. Hold wire

at 1/2" from end with round nose pliers and fold wire over round nose to form a loop.
2. Add a diamond shaped black matte bead over both wires. *(Fig. 6)* Form a wire loop on the other end of bead *(Fig. 7)* and wrap wire tightly around loop. Clip ending wire tail as needed.
3. Prepare 14 beads units as in steps 1 and 2 (all for necklace).

Assemble the Necklace:

Connect beads with jump rings in this order: copper spiral, black diamond bead, antique copper spiral, black diamond bead, repeat until all are used. Necklace will slip over your head.

Assemble the Earrings:

1. Thread a black diamond bead onto an eyepin. Make a loop in the end of eyepin, using needlenose pliers. Repeat for second black bead on eyepin.
2. Using jump rings, attach a copper spiral to each fish hook earwire. Attach a black diamond bead to bottom of each copper spiral. *(Fig. 8)*

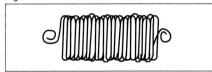
Fig. 1

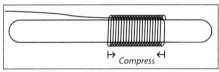
Fig. 2

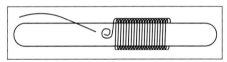
Fig. 3

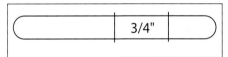
Fig. 4

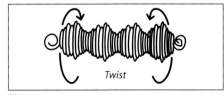
Twist
Fig. 5

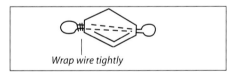
Fig. 6

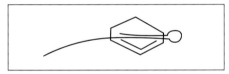
Wrap wire tightly
Fig. 7

Fig. 8

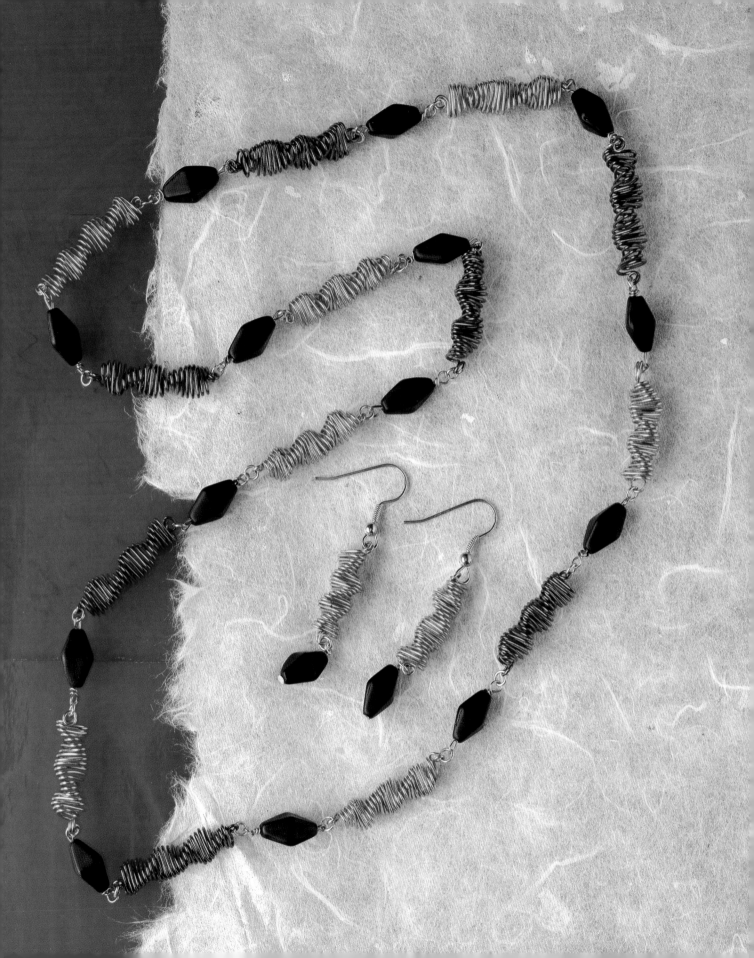

Spiral Wreaths
Earrings

Designed by Patty Cox

Finished size of Earrings (excluding findings): 1-1/4" long (1" diam. wreaths)

You Will Need

Supplies:
Dark green wire, 22 gauge
Two 4mm red beads
Mini craft stick
Set of fish hook earring findings

Tools:
Round nose pliers
Needlenose pliers

Follow These Steps

Form the Spirals:

1. Mark two lines on the mini craft stick 1-3/4" apart. *(Fig. 1)*
2. Leaving a 1" wire tail, wrap wire around craft stick between marks. Compress wraps tightly in order to make as many wraps as possible without overlapping wire. *(Fig. 2)*
3. Trim end of wire to 1" beyond wraps. Slide wire off craft stick.
4. Gently twist wire into a spiral with your fingers. *(Fig. 3)*

Assemble Earrings:

1. Bring the 1" wire tails together, forming a circle with the spiraled wire. Add a red bead on both wire tails as one. *(Fig. 4)* Twist wires tails together.
2. Trim wire tails to about 3/8". Form them (together) into a loop, using round nose pliers.
3. Attach a fish hook earwire to top loop of each wreath.❝

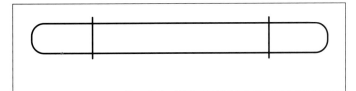

Fig. 1

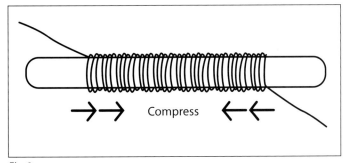

Fig. 2

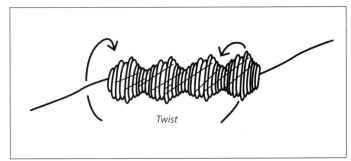

Twist

Fig. 3

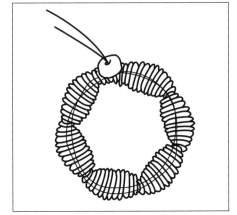

Fig. 4

Coiled Trees
Earrings
(Pictured on page 31)

Designed by Patty Cox

Finished length of Earrings (excluding findings): 1"

You Will Need
Supplies:
Green wire, 22 gauge
Gold wire, 32 gauge
Red seed beads
Set of gold fish hook earring findings

Tools:
Power drill
Buss wire, 16 gauge: 10" length
Needlenose pliers

Follow These Steps
Make the Coils:
1. Insert a 10" length of buss wire into drill. Add the end of 22-gauge green wire and one yard of 32-gauge gold wire in the drill. Thread about 12 red seed beads on the 32-gauge wire. Allow the spool of 22-gauge wire to drop. Close and secure wire ends in drill. *(Fig. 1)*
2. Switch drill speed to slow. Slowly run drill and pinch wires, allowing the 22-gauge and 32- gauge wires to coil around buss wire. Compress coiled wire tightly against drill.
3. Bring a seed bead up against buss wire, coil wires for about 1/2", and add another seed bead. *(Fig. 2)* Continue coiling 22 gauge wire to a 5" length. Remove coil from buss wire.
4. Insert a 7" length of 22 gauge green wire through coil. Twist ends of this wire and coiled wire together to secure. *(Fig. 3)*
5. Repeat steps 1-4 for another 5" coil.

Assemble Earrings:
1. Wrap the 5" coil around a pencil. *(Fig. 4)*
2. Form coil into a triangular tree shape by closing the coil at the top of tree and opening coil at the base of tree. *(Fig. 5)*
3. Form a loop in wire ends at top of tree. *(Fig. 5)* Secure other wire end to coil around tree base.
4. Attach fish hook earwire to tree top loop.
5. Repeat steps 1-4 for second earring.❲

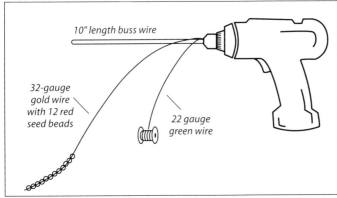

Fig. 1

10" length buss wire

32-gauge gold wire with 12 red seed beads

22 gauge green wire

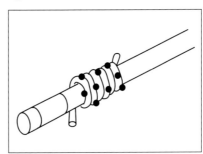

Fig. 3

Twist wire ends

Insert 7" length 22-gauge wire.

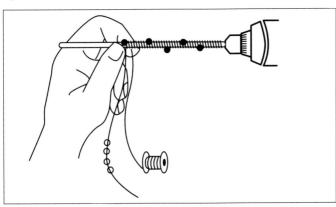

Fig. 2

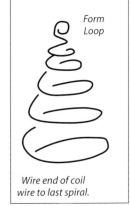

Fig. 4

Fig. 5

Form Loop

Wire end of coil wire to last spiral.

Copper Spiral
Stickpin
(Pictured on page 35)

Designed by Patty Cox

Finished Size of Pin: 1-1/8" wide x 3" long

You Will Need

Supplies:

Copper wire, 16 gauge
Copper wire, 28 gauge
Copper seed beads
Matte black seed beads
One black spaghetti bead
Two bell beads, painted black
Stickpin
Jewelry glue

Tools:

Flat coil maker (see "Constructing a Flat Coil" in General Instructions)
Round nose pliers
Needlenose pliers

Follow These Steps

Making the Coil:

1. Cut a 12" length of 16 gauge copper wire. Using coil maker, make a 1-1/8" flat coil, leaving a 2-1/2" tail. *(Fig. 1)*
2. Bend the tail into an irregular zigzag, using needlenose pliers. *(Fig. 2)* Bend the end of the tail into an open coil, using round nose pliers.

Making the Beaded Portion:

1. Cut a 12" length of 28 gauge copper wire. Hold wire 1/2" from end with round nose pliers. Fold wire over round nose to form a loop. *(Fig. 3)*

2. Add the black spaghetti bead over both wires. Form a loop on other end of bead and wrap wire tightly around loop. *(Fig. 4)*
3. Wrap wire around spaghetti bead, then wrap wire tightly around other loop. *(Fig. 5)* Clip end.
4. Thread seed beads and bells on 28 gauge wire as shown. *(Fig. 6)* Make two strands. Attach wire ends to loops on spaghetti bead. *(Fig. 6)*

Assemble Pin:

1. Wire spaghetti bead to 16 gauge copper wire just below the flat coil. *(Fig. 7)*
2. Glue stickpin on back of coil.

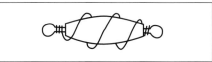

Fig. 4

Fig. 5

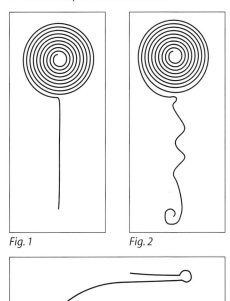

Fig. 1

Fig. 2

Fig. 3

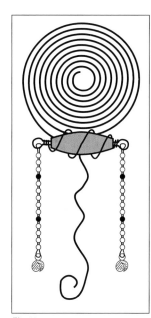

Fig. 6   Fig. 7

Spiral Disk Collage
Fashion Pin

Designed by Patty Cox

Finished Size of Pin: 1-3/8" wide x 2-1/2" long

You Will Need

Supplies:
Thin solder wire, 3" length
Buss wire, 16 gauge
Gold wire, 28 gauge
Silver wire, 32 gauge
Wire mesh, 40 gauge
Black spaghetti bead
Round red bead, 6mm
Pin back

Tools:
Flat coil maker (see "Constructing a Flat Coil" in General Instructions)
Round nose pliers
Needlenose pliers

Follow These Steps

1. Cut a 12" length of 16 gauge buss wire. Make a 1-1/4" diameter flat coil.
2. Cut a 12" length of gold wire. Hold wire 1/2" from end with round nose pliers. Fold wire over round nose to form a loop. Thread black spaghetti bead over both wires. (Fig. 1) Form a loop on the other end of bead and wrap wire tightly around loop.
3. Wrap wire around bead. (Fig. 2) Wrap wire tightly around other loop and clip excess wire. (Fig. 3)
4. Cut two wire mesh pieces, using patterns given. Fold raw edges to back. Crimp folds with needlenose pliers.

5. Cut a 3" length of solder wire. Bend it into an open coil, using round nose pliers as shown. (Fig. 4) Loop ends of the spaghetti bead over this wire as shown.

6. Wire all pieces together with 32 gauge wire as shown in diagram and photo of finished pin. (Fig. 4)
7. Wire pin back to backside of coil.◖

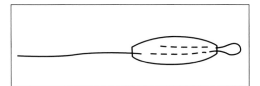

Fig. 1

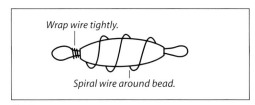

Fig. 2

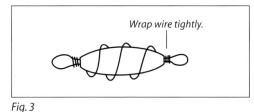

Fig. 3

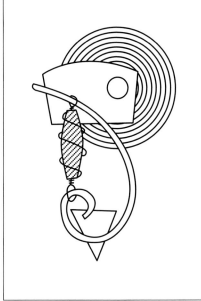

Fig. 4

Cut 1 each
#40 wire mesh

—— Fold edges to back.

—— Flatten folds with needlenose pliers.

Pattern

Copper Sprial Stickpen, instructions on page 33

Sprial Disk Collage

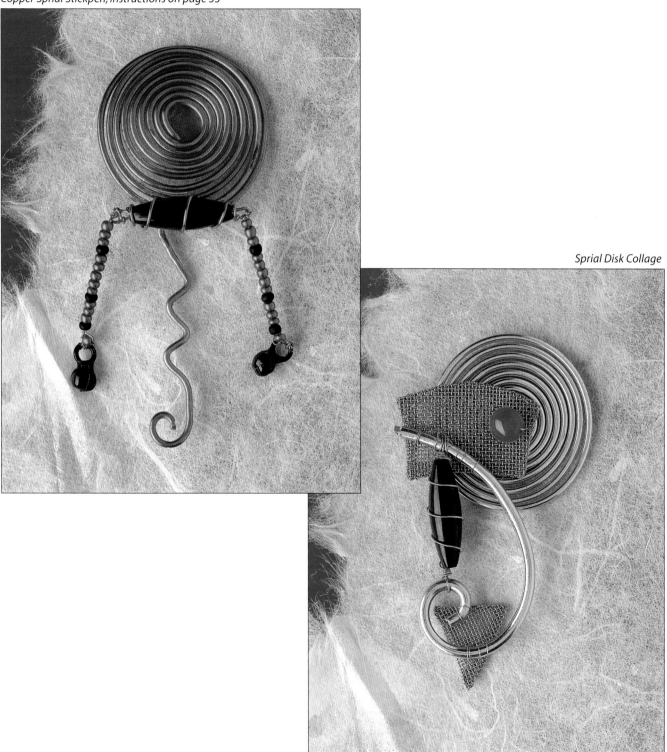

Blue Coiled Beads
ID Chain

Designed by Patty Cox

Finished Length of Necklace: 24" + 1"
   coiled dangle

You Will Need
Supplies:

Blue wire, 24 gauge

Fingernail clip earring finding

Tools:

Power drill

Buss wire, 16 gauge: 10" length

Round nose pliers

Needlenose pliers

Follow These Steps
Make the Coiled Beads:

1. Insert a 10" piece of buss wire and the end of the 24 gauge blue wire into drill. Allow spool of 24 gauge wire to drop. Close and secure wire ends in drill. (Fig. 1)

2. Coil the wire to a 1" length of coiled wire, following directions in "How to Coil Wire With a Drill" in General Instructions. Remove coil from buss wire. Trim end of 24 gauge wire 3" from coil. (Fig. 2)

3. Hold wire tail next to coil with round nose pliers and form loop. (Fig. 3) Wrap wire tightly around loop. Bring wire tail through coil to other side and form another loop. (Fig. 4) Wrap wire tightly around loop. Trim other wire tail to 1/2". Tuck this end inside coiled bead. (Fig. 5)

Assemble Chain:

1. Loop wire end of one bead through loop of next bead. (Fig. 6) Continue until all but one coiled beads are used.

2. Wire a fingernail clip earring finding to remaining coiled bead. Connect chain ends to other end of this coil. (Fig. 7) Attach ID to fingernail clip earring finding at bottom of coiled bead dangle.❖

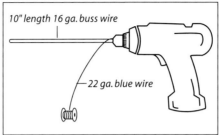

10" length 16 ga. buss wire

22 ga. blue wire

Fig. 1

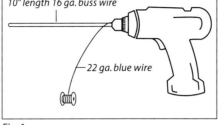

1" coil

Trim wire to 3" beyond coil.

Fig. 2

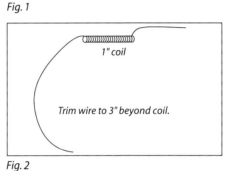

Form loop.

Wrap wire around loop.

Fig. 3

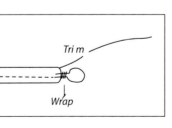

Tri m

Wrap

Fig. 4

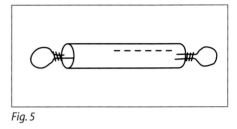

Fig. 5

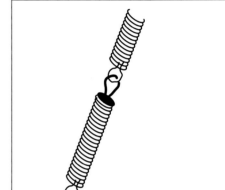

Fig. 6

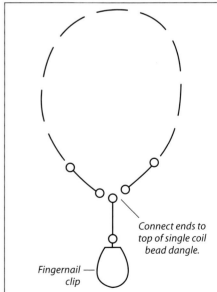

Connect ends to top of single coil bead dangle.

Fingernail clip

Fig.7

Red Spiral Twists
Necklace/Glasses Holder

Designed by Patty Cox

Finished Length of Necklace: 35-1/2"

You Will Need

Supplies:
Red wire, 22 gauge
Gold wire, 24 gauge
Red beads, 6mm
Gold beads, 4mm
Alphabet beads (to spell your initials or name)
Necklace chain: one 7" length and two 2" lengths
Rubber glasses holders

Tools:
Mini craft stick
Round nose pliers
Needlenose pliers

Follow These Steps

Form the Spiral Beads:
1. Mark two lines 1-1/4" apart on a mini craft stick. (Fig. 1)
2. Place a 3" tail of the wire along the edge of the craft stick. Wrap wire over tail and around craft stick. Compress wraps tightly to fit as many wraps as possible between the marks without overlapping wire. (Fig. 2)
3. Trim the 3" wire tail to approximately 3/8" Form into a loop using round nose pliers. (Fig. 3)
4. Slide wire off of craft stick. Using needlenose pliers, twist a loop in the other end of wire. (Fig. 4)
5. Gently twist wire into a spiral with your fingers. (Fig. 5)
6. Repeat for each spiral bead. Make eight spiral beads.

Round Beads:
1. Cut a 4" length of gold wire. Hold the wire with round nose pliers 1/2" from its end. Fold wire over round nose to form a loop. (Fig. 6)

2. Add a 4mm gold bead, a 6mm red bead, and another 4mm gold bead over both wires. Form a wire loop on other end of beads.
3. Wrap wire around all beads, then wrap wire tightly around second loop. (Fig. 7) Clip wire tail as needed.
4. Repeat steps 1-3 for each group of round beads. Make 11 round bead units.

Alphabet Beads:
1. Cut a 4" length of gold wire. Hold the wire with round nose pliers 1/2" from its end. Fold wire over round nose to form a loop. (Fig. 6)
2. Add alphabet beads over both wires. Form a wire loop on other end of beads. Wrap wire tightly around second loop. Clip wire tail as needed.

3. Repeat steps 1 and 2 for another identical group, but reverse the order of letters.

Assemble Necklace/Glasses Holder:
1. Alternate spiral wire beads and round bead units, starting with a round bead unit. Connect them with jump rings. After three round bead groups and two spiral wire beads, add the alphabet beads, then repeat the first sequence.
2. Connect a 7" necklace chain section (will be at necklace center back), then repeat the whole bead sequence for other side of necklace. (Fig. 8) Attach 2" necklace chain sections at each end of necklace.
3. Attach rubber glasses holders at each chain end. (Fig. 8)◖

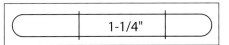

1-1/4"

Fig. 1

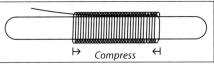

Compress

Fig. 2

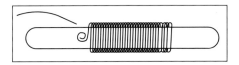

Fig. 3

Fig. 4

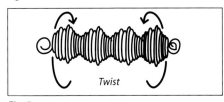

Twist

Fig. 5

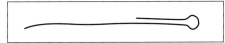

Fig. 6

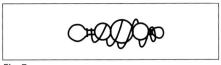

Fig. 7

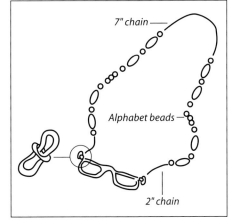

7" chain

Alphabet beads

2" chain

Fig. 8

Spirals and Roses
Headband

Designed by Patty Cox

Finished length of Headband Decoration: 10"

You Will Need

Supplies:
Dark green wire, 22 gauge
Red wire, 20 gauge
Silver wire, 32 gauge
Silver headband

Tools:
Flat coil maker (see "Constructing a Flat Coil" in General Instructions)
Power drill
Buss wire, 16 gauge: 10" length
Round nose pliers
Needlenose pliers

Follow These Steps

Make the Coils:

1. Insert a 10" length of buss wire and the end of dark green 22 gauge wire into drill. Allow spool of 22 gauge wire to drop. *(Fig. 1)* Close and secure wire ends in drill.
2. Coil 22 gauge wire to a 5" coiled length, following directions in "How to Coil Wire With a Drill" in General Instructions. Remove coil from buss wire.
3. Insert a 7" length of 22 gauge dark green wire through coil and twist wire ends together to secure. *(Fig. 2)*

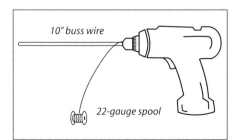

Fig. 1

4. Spiral-wrap 5" coil around buss wire. *(Fig. 3)*
5. Follow steps 1-4 for other spiraled coils. Make four spiraled coils.

Making the Coiled Roses:

1. Form three 1/2" diameter flat coils with 20 gauge red wire, using the flat coil maker.
2. Bend beginning end of wire into a loop. Cut away finishing end of wire. *(Figs. 4 and 5)*
3. Following the pattern given, bend outline of three sets of leaves with 22 gauge dark green wire. Twist wire ends together on each set.
4. Wire leaves to backs of coiled roses (red flat coils)

Assemble the Headband:

1. With 32 gauge silver wire, tightly secure green spiraled coils to headband. *(Fig. 6)*
2. Wire coiled roses between the dark green spiraled coils. ◖

Fig. 2

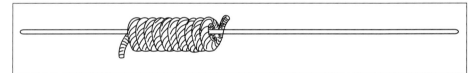

Fig. 3

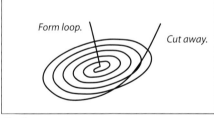

Fig. 4

Fig. 5

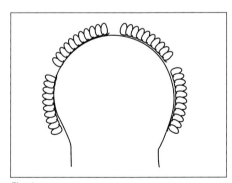

Fig. 6

Leaf Pattern

Turquoise & Plum Coiled Twists
Choker and Earrings

Designed by Patty Cox

Finished Length of Choker: 18"
Finished Length of Earring (excluding finding): 2-1/4"

You Will Need
Supplies:
Peacock blue (turquoise) wire, 26 gauge
Plum wire, 26 gauge
Five turquoise fiberglass beads, 8mm
Six purple fiberglass beads, 6mm
Eighteen clear AB (rainbow) acrylic beads, 4mm
Beading thread or beading wire, 24" length
Silver necklace clasp
Set of silver fish hook earring findings

Tools:
Beading needle (if using beading thread instead of wire)
Power drill
Buss wire, 10" length
Round nose pliers
Needlenose pliers

Follow These Steps
Make the Twisted Coils for Choker:
1. Insert a 10" length of buss wire and the end of 26 gauge wire into drill. Allow spool of 26 gauge wire to drop. (Fig. 1) Close and secure wire ends in drill.
2. Coil until coiled wire measures 2-1/2" long, following directions in "How to Coil Wire With a Drill" in General Instructions. Remove coil from buss wire. (Fig. 2)
3. Twist wire ends together, forming a loop. (Fig. 3)
4. Twist the loop to form a coiled twist bead. (Fig. 4) Trim wire ends and tuck them into bead.
5. Repeat steps 1-4 for each coiled twist bead. Make five peacock blue beads and five plum beads.

Assemble Choker:
1. Attach necklace clasp to one end of beading thread or wire.
2. Thread a purple fiberglass bead next to clasp. Then thread the following beads: peacock blue coiled twist bead, clear bead, turquoise bead, clear bead, plum coiled twist bead, clear bead, purple bead, clear bead. Repeat this order until all are used. Attack ending wire to other end of necklace clasp.

Make Earrings:
1. Make two 5" plum coils in the same manner as the 2-1/2" coils made for choker.
2. Twist coils to form a 2" to 2-1/4" spiral twist bead.
3. Trim wire ends to 1/2" and form a loop with them.
4. Attach a fish hook earwire to wire loop of twisted bead.
5. Repeat steps 1-4 for second earring.

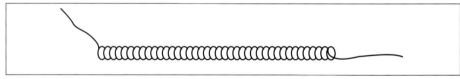

Fig. 2

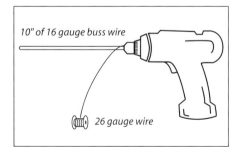

Fig. 1
10" of 16 gauge buss wire
26 gauge wire

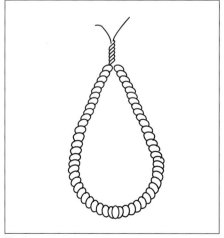

Fig. 3

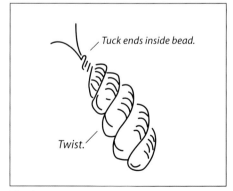
Tuck ends inside bead.
Twist.

Fig. 4

Coils and Beads
Pendant and Earrings

Designed by Diana Thomas

Finished Length of Pendant: 2"
Finished Length of Earrings: 2"

You Will Need
Supplies:
Antique copper (brown) wire, 14 gauge
Six black cloisonné beads, 12mm
Three black cloisonnÈ beads, 8mm
Four black E beads
Three black seed beads
Three gold eyepins, 2"
Three gold headpins, 1"
Two gold crimp beads
Three gold jump rings
Lobster claw necklace clasp
Black satin (rattail) cord, 18" length (or
    desired length)
Set of gold fish hook earring findings

Tools:
Dowel, 3/8" diam.
Wire cutters
Round nose pliers
Needlenose pliers
File

Follow These Steps
Make the Coils:
1. Tightly wrap wire around the dowel until you have a coil 5/8" long (nine wraps). *(Fig. 1)* Snip the wire at each end with wire cutters. Slip coil off dowel. File cut edges until smooth.
2. Repeat for two more coils (three total). Two are for earrings, one for pendant.

Make Coil/Bead Units:
1. Thread the following onto eyepin: E bead, 8mm bead, coil, 8mm, and E bead.
2. Leave 3/8" of eyepin to form loop and cut off excess with wire cutters. Form loop at end of eyepin with round nose pliers.
3. Thread an 8mm bead and seed bead onto headpin.
4. Leave 3/8" on headpin and cut off excess. Form loop at end of headpin with round nose pliers.
5. Open loop of headpin and slip loop of eyepin onto it. Squeeze shut with pliers.
6. Repeat steps 1-5 for two more coil/bead units.

Assemble Pendant:
1. Close a crimp bead over each end of satin cord, using pliers.
2. Attach clasp to one crimp bead with a jump ring.
3. Attach a jump ring to crimp bead on other end of cord.
4. Attach pendant to cord with a jump ring.

Assemble Earrings:
1. Open eye of earwire and slip eye at second end of coil/bead unit onto it. Squeeze shut with pliers.
2. Repeat for second earring.◖

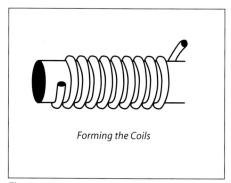

Forming the Coils

Fig. 1

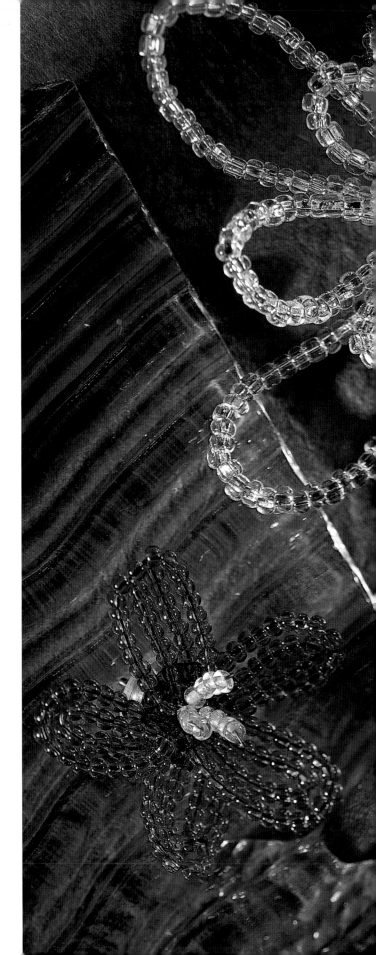

Bead and Pearl Woven Jewelry

Wire is perfect for weaving beads, and woven bead jewelry is delightful. Skilled artisans know it. And American Indians knew it centuries ago.

The jewelry in this section features this fun and beautiful technique—solid areas of woven beads on wire. Using beading wire relieves you of the needle and thimble you need when using thread, and the projects will be stronger and more durable besides.

Blue Angel
Stickpin

Designed by Patty Cox

Finished Size of Pin (Angel Portion): 3/4"
wide x 7/8" high

You Will Need

Supplies:
Gold beading wire, 32 gauge
Transparent peach faceted bead, 4mm
Three gold seed beads
34 turquoise seed beads
22 clear seed beads
Gold disk, 14mm
Gold stickpin

Tools:
Round nose pliers
Needlenose pliers

Follow These Steps

Angel Body:
1. Cut a 24" length of 32 gauge gold wire. Wrap center of wire around gold disk. (Fig. 1)
2. Insert wire strands—arms of angel—through the 4mm faceted bead.
3. On one wire, thread three turquoise seed beads and one gold seed bead. Bring wire around gold bead, then back through turquoise beads. Repeat with other wire. (Fig. 1)
4. Thread one turquoise seed bead on one wire. Run the other wire through the same seed bead in the opposite direction. (Fig. 1) Pull wires tightly.
5. Thread two turquoise seed beads on one wire. Run other wire through same seed beads in opposite direction. (Fig. 2) Pull wires tightly.
6. Continue in the same manner as step 5, adding one additional seed bead on each row to form angel's dress. End with a row

of seven seed beads. Run wire ends through previous row of seed beads and clip wire ends. (Fig. 2)

Angel Wings:
1. Cut a 12" length of 32 gauge gold beading wire. Thread 11 clear seed beads on wire.
2. Form a loop with the beads and twist wires together.

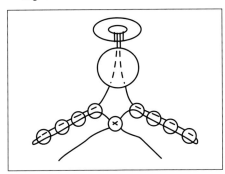

Fig. 1

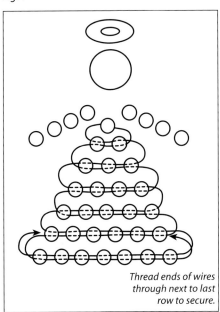

Thread ends of wires
through next to last
row to secure.

Fig. 2

3. Repeat steps 1 and 2 for other wing. (Fig. 3)
4. Wrap wires around angel's neck. Twist wires and clip ends.
5. Wire stickpin on angel's back.❮

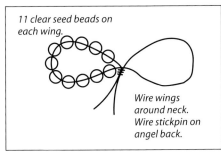

11 clear seed beads on
each wing.

Wire wings
around neck.
Wire stickpin on
angel back.

Fig. 3

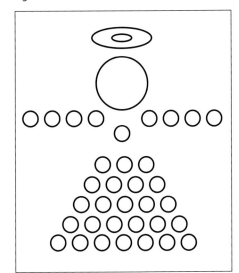

Beading diagram

Pictured (clockwise from top right): Pearl Angel Pin, instructions on page 50; Pearl Victorian Lady Pin, instructions on page 51; Blue Angel Stickpin, instructions on page 48

Pearl Angel
Fashion Pin
(Pictured on page 49)

Designed by Patty Cox

Finished Size of Pin: 2" wide x 2-1/2" high

You Will Need

Supplies:

Gold wire, 28 gauge
gold wire, 24 gauge
Pearls, 4mm
Pearls, 3mm
Peach pearl, 8mm
Pearl oat bead, 3mm x 6mm
Gold seed beads
Gold disk, 14mm
Pin back

Tools:

T-pin
Round nose pliers
Needlenose pliers

Follow These Steps

Halo, Head & Neck:

1. Cut a 36" length of 28 gauge gold wire. Thread a gold seed bead on center of wire. This will be top of angel.
2. On both wires, add a 14mm gold disk, three 6" lengths of 28 gauge gold wire (insert between wires from disk—these wires will later make hair), an 8mm peach bead, then a gold seed bead. (Fig. 1)

Arms:

1. Separate wires from previous gold seed bead. On one wire, thread a pearl oat bead, a 3mm pearl, a pearl oat bead, then a gold seed bead. Run wire around gold seed bead, then back through all beads. (Fig. 1)
2. Repeat on other wire for other arm.
3. Thread wires through a single 4mm pearl in opposite directions. Pull wires tightly.

Dress:

1. Add two 4mm pearls to one wire. Thread the other wire through same pearls in opposite direction. (Fig. 1) Pull wires tightly.
2. Add three 4mm pearls to one wire. Thread the other wire through same pearls in opposite direction. Pull wires tightly.
3. Continue adding rows of skirt according to Fig. 1. Secure wire ends by running them through the previous row of pearls. Clip ends.

Hair:

Coil the hair wires on each side around a T-pin for six curls.

Wings:

1. Form wings with 24 gauge gold wire, following pattern given.
2. Wire wings and a pin back to angel back.

Wing pattern

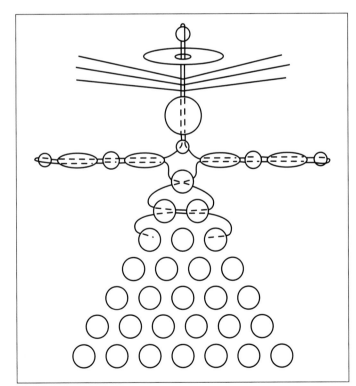

Fig. 1

Pearl Victorian Lady
Fashion Pin
(Pictured on page 49)

Designed by Patty Cox

Finished Size of Pin: 1-1/4" wide x 2-1/4" high

You Will Need
Supplies:
Gold wire, 28 gauge
Pearls, 4mm
Three 4mm peach pearls
One 8mm peach pearl
Pearl oat beads, 3mm x 6mm
White rondel bead
Gold seed beads
Gold disk, 14mm
Pin back

Tools:
T-pin
Needlenose pliers

Follow These Steps
Hat, Head & Neck:
1. Cut a 36" length of 28 gauge gold wire. Thread a gold seed bead on center of wire. This will be top of angel.
2. On both wires, add three 6" lengths of 28 gauge gold wire (insert between wires from disk— these wires will later make hat top), a 14mm gold disk, an 8mm peach bead, then a 4mm peach pearl. *(Fig. 1)*

Arms:
1. Separate wires from previous 4mm peach pearl. On one wire, thread a pearl oat bead, a 3mm pearl, a pearl oat bead, a 4mm peach pearl, then a gold seed bead. Run wire around gold seed bead, then back through all beads. *(Fig. 1)*
2. Repeat on other wire for other arm.
3. Thread wires through a single 4mm pearl in opposite directions. Pull wires tightly.

Dress:
1. Add two 4mm pearls to one wire. Thread the other wire through same pearls in opposite direction. *(Fig. 1)* Pull wires tightly.
2. Add three 4mm pearls to one wire. Thread the other wire through same pearls in opposite direction. Pull wires tightly.
3. Continue adding rows of skirt according to *Fig. 1*. Secure wire ends by running them through the previous row of pearls. Clip ends.

Hat Top:
1. Coil the hat top wires on each side around a T-pin for six coiled decorations.
2. Position and roll coils together in a cluster.

Umbrella:
1. Cut a 12" length of 28 gauge gold wire.
2. Thread on a gold seed bead to center of wire. This will be bottom of umbrella. Fold the wire around the seed bead.
3. Thread the following beads on both wires as one: three gold seed beads, three pearl oat beads, white rondel bead, and two gold seed beads.
4. Twist wire end around lady's left wrist.
5. Wire pin back to backside of lady.

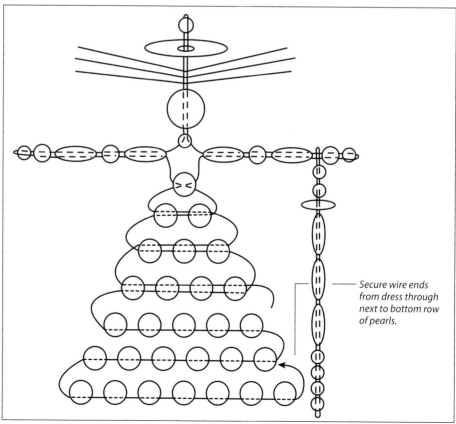

Secure wire ends from dress through next to bottom row of pearls.

Fig. 1

Ring With Wings
Finger Butterfly

Designed by Patty Cox

Finished Size of Butterfly: 7/8" wide
  (when flattened)

You Will Need

Supplies:
Gold beading wire, 32 gauge
Clear seed beads
Black matte seed beads
Transparent turquoise seed beads
Transparent cobalt blue seed beads

Tools:
Needlenose pliers

Follow These Steps

Ring Circlet & Butterfly Body:

1. Begin at center top of ring with butterfly body. Cut two 36" lengths of wire and thread both wires through seven black seed beads. Separate wires on each end of beads. You will work each side of circlet separately. Start on one side with a wire from each end of seed beads.

2. Thread six clear seed beads onto one of these wires for this side of circlet. Thread the other wire through the same beads from the opposite direction. *(Fig. 1)*

3. Continue in the same manner for four more rows, using one less bead on each row. Follow the beading diagram. *(Fig. 1)*

4. Continue, adding as many two-bead rows as needed to fit your finger. Remember, this is just half of the circlet.

5. Repeat the same procedure on other side of butterfly body beads.

6. Form the beading into a circlet. Thread the wires from one end of one side through the last row of other side in opposite directions, and vice versa. *(Fig. 2)* Pull wires tightly. Thread wires backwards through several rows (toward wider part of ring) on both sides of circlet to secure wire ends. Clip excess wire.

Make Butterfly Wings:

1. Begin at outside of upper wing. Shaded circles on diagrams represent cobalt blue seed beads; other circles represent turquoise seed beads. Cut a 36" length of 32 gauge wire. Thread four cobalt blue seed beads to center of wire. Take each wire end to other end of beads and thread it back through; the wires will be threading through beads in opposite directions. *(Fig. 3)*

2. For next row add five seed beads—cobalt blue beads on the ends of row and turquoise beads in middle of row. Thread these beads onto one wire, then take other wire through same beads in the opposite direction. *(Fig. 4)*

3. Continue in this manner, following the beading pattern in *Fig. 5,* until upper wing is completed. Then with wire from upper wing, bead the lower wing following Fig. 5.

4. Weave wire through bead back to center as shown in *Fig. 6.*

5. Make second wing in the same manner, reversing the direction in which you are working.

6. Wire wings through butterfly body on center of circlet. Secure wire through an adjacent row on each side. Clip excess wire. ❧

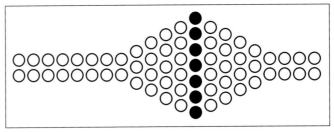

Fig. 1

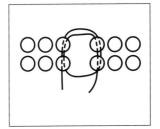

Fig. 2

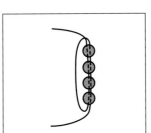

Fig. 3

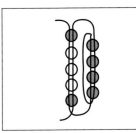

Fig. 4

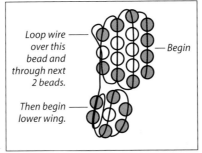

Loop wire over this bead and through next 2 beads.

Then begin lower wing.

Begin

Fig. 5

Weave wires through beads back to center.

Fig. 6

Pictured (clockwise from top): Blue Beaded Flowers Earrings, instructions on page 54; Ring With Wings Finger Butterfly; Blue Beaded Beauty Hair Comb, instructions on page 55

Blue Beaded Flowers
Earrings
(Pictured on page 53)

Designed by Patty Cox

Finished size of earring: 1-1/4" diam.
(when flattened)

You Will Need
Supplies:
Beading wire, 32 gauge
Blue seed beads
Pale yellow seed beads
Post earring backs
Clear epoxy glue

Tools:
Needlenose pliers

Follow These Steps
Make Flower Petals:
1. Cut a 12" length of 32 gauge wire. Thread 15 blue seed beads on wire. (Fig. 1)
2. Loop beads and wire to form inner petal and twist wires together. (Fig. 2)
3. Add approximately 22 beads on one of the wires. Loop this strand of beads around inner petal. (Fig. 3) Twist wires together.
4. Repeat steps 1-3 for remaining petals. Make ten petals total—five for each earring. (Fig. 4)

Make Stamens:
1. Cut an 8" length of 32 gauge wire. Thread a pale yellow seed bead to center of wire. Fold wire over bead. Add three pale yellow seed beads onto both wires as one. *(Fig. 5)* Twist wire ends together.
2. Repeat step 1 for other stamens. Make six stamens—three per flower.

Assemble Earrings:
1. Hold five flower petals around four stamens. Twist all wire ends together. *(Fig. 6)*
2. Trim wire ends below twists. Wrap twisted wire into a coil. Glue earring back on twisted coil. *(Fig. 7)*
3. Repeat steps 1 and 2 for second earring.

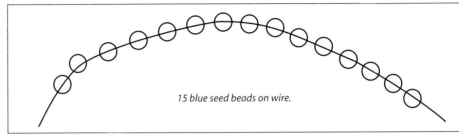

15 blue seed beads on wire.

Fig. 1

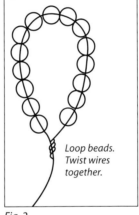

Loop beads. Twist wires together.

Fig. 2

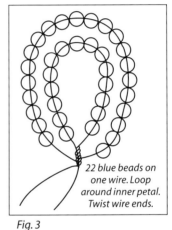

22 blue beads on one wire. Loop around inner petal. Twist wire ends.

Fig. 3

Make 5 petals per flower

Fig. 4

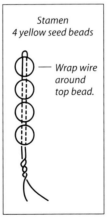

Stamen
4 yellow seed beads

Wrap wire around top bead.

Fig. 5

Twist wire ends together

Fig. 6

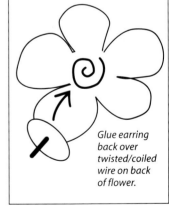

Glue earring back over twisted/coiled wire on back of flower.

Fig. 7

Blue Beaded Beauty
Hair Comb
(Pictured on page 53)

Designed by Diana Thomas

Finished Width of Comb: 2-1/2"

You Will Need
Supplies:
Lavender wire, 28 gauge
Pkg. purple seed beads
Clear plastic hair comb, 2-1/2" wide

Tools:
Wire cutters
Needlenose pliers

Follow These Steps
1. Cut a 26" length of wire. Hold tip of wire at top right end of hair comb with pliers. Wrap wire tightly around end of comb three times. *(Fig. 1)*
2. Thread seven beads onto wire.
3. Wrap beaded wire from back of comb over top to front of comb, placing the beads on front of comb.
4. Holding beads against comb, wrap wire between teeth of comb. *(Fig. 2)*
5. Repeat steps 2-4 to other end of comb. There are two wraps in each space between teeth.
6. Wrap wire around comb three times to secure. Trim excess wire and tighten end of wire against comb with pliers.❆

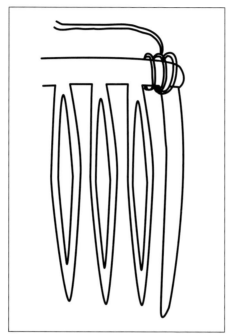

Fig. 1

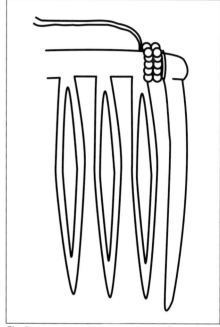

Fig. 2

Kindred Spirit Woven Beads
Earrings

Designed by Patty Cox

Finished Length of Earring (excluding finding): 2"

You Will Need

Supplies:
Gold wire, 32 gauge
Two 4mm peach faceted beads
Seed beads: gold, turquoise, black, orange, yellow, and red
Set of gold fish hook earring findings

Tools:
Round nose pliers
Needlenose pliers

Follow These Steps

Top Loop & Head:

1. Cut a 36" length of 32 gauge gold wire. Thread six gold seed beads to center of wire. Form into a circle and thread both wires through a black seed bead. (Fig. 1) Take both wires through beads of top loop again (in opposite directions) to reinforce, then back through black bead.

2. Thread peach faceted bead on both wires. (Fig. 1)

Arms:

1. Separate wires out to each side. Thread three black seed beads and one gold seed bead on one wire. Bring wire around gold bead, then take it back through black beads. (Fig. 2)

2. Repeat with other wire for other arm.

3. Thread a black seed bead onto one wire. Run other wire through same black seed bead in the opposite direction. (Fig. 2) Pull wires tightly.

Dress:

1. Thread a black, a turquoise, then a black seed bead on one wire. Run end of other wire through these seed beads in the opposite direction. Pull wires tightly. (Fig. 3)

2. Continue adding beads on each row, then decreasing beads on each row, adding rows by the same procedure as in step 1. Follow the beading diagram (Fig. 3) for bead colors.

3. Run beading wire ends through previous rows of seed beads to secure. Clip excess wire ends.

4. Attach fish hook earwires through top loops.❦

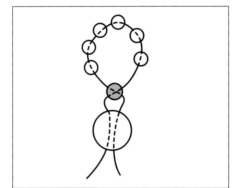

Fig. 1

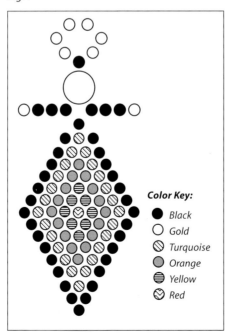

Color Key:

● Black
○ Gold
⊘ Turquoise
⬤ Orange
⊜ Yellow
⊗ Red

Fig. 3 — Beading diagram

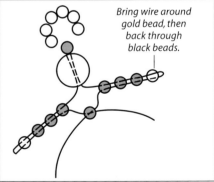

Bring wire around gold bead, then back through black beads.

Fig. 2

Snow Crystal Flower
Fashion Pin

Designed by Diana Thomas

Finished Size of Pin: 2" x 2"

You Will Need
Supplies:
Silver beading wire, 24 gauge
Silver beading wire, 32 gauge
Pkg. crystal seed beads
Silver pin back, 1"

Tools:
Wire cutters
Needlenose pliers

Follow These Steps
Make First Layer of (Large) Petals:
1. Cut a 34" length of 24 gauge wire. Crimp one end of wire to prevent beads from sliding off.
2. Thread beads onto wire, covering entire length except for 1/2" on other end. Crimp this end.
3. Cut a 20" length of 32 gauge wire for a tie wire..
4. Form first petal by looping one end of beaded wire back to itself to form a 1-1/2" long petal. Wrap end twice with 32 gauge tie wire. *(Fig. 1)*
5. Working clockwise, repeat step 4 to form three more petals. Connect first and fourth petals together at base.

Make Second Layer of (Medium) Petals:
1. Bring beaded wire forward. Form first petal by looping beaded wire back on itself to form a 1-1/8" long petal. Wrap end twice with tie wire.
2. Working clockwise, repeat step 1 to form three more medium petals. Connect first and fourth medium petals together at base

Make Third Layer of (Small) Petals:
1. Bring beaded wire forward. Form first petal by looping one end of beaded wire back on itself to form a 3/4" long petal. Wrap end twice with tie wire.
2. Working clockwise, repeat step 1 to form three more small petals. Connect first and fourth small petals together at base.

Make Flower Center:
1. Form remaining beaded wire into a flat coil in center of petals, making sure that the crimped end is folded under coil to hide it.
2. Secure coil to center of flower by bringing tie wire over edge and through center on two sides. Cut off excess tie wire. Flatten end of tie wire to back of flower with pliers.
3. Wire pin back to back of beaded flower.

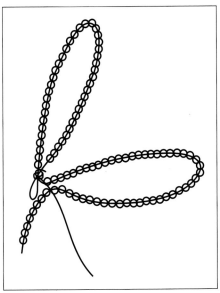

Fig. 1

Multifaceted Personalities Jewelry

With all the shapes of beads on the market today, beads can be strung on wire to represent a host of characters. This section presents a variety of them. There are special day personalities such as Santa and a bride and groom...and everyday people like Ben and Betty...and the irrepressible teen group with a cheerleader, teen boy and girl, and soccer boy and girl. And, of course, there are babies.

The characters can be used as pins by adding a pin back or as a necklace pendant. The smaller ones can be used as charms on necklaces, pins, or bracelets or as earrings. They can also be used in other ways such as gift package decorations or favors.

You'll enjoy the creativity of fashioning characters from beads on wire.

Santa
Jolly Personality

Designed by Patty Cox

Finished Size: 3" long

You Will Need
Supplies:
Gold wire, 28 gauge
Black seed beads
White seed beads
Peach pearl, 8mm
Two red E beads
Four red spaghetti beads
Five white rondel beads
Three red bell beads
Four black beads, 4mm
Six white beads, 4mm
Black button or disk, 1/2" diam.

Tools:
Wire cutters
Needlenose pliers

Follow These Steps
1. All multifaceted characters are made basically the same way. Follow beading charts and for more details, refer to the Betty and Ben projects on pages 68 and 70 which use the same procedures.
2. Add beard after Santa's body has been assembled. Thread five 4mm white beads on an 8" length wire. Thread wire ends through hat to top. *(Fig. 2)* Twist wire ends together, then clip ends.❮

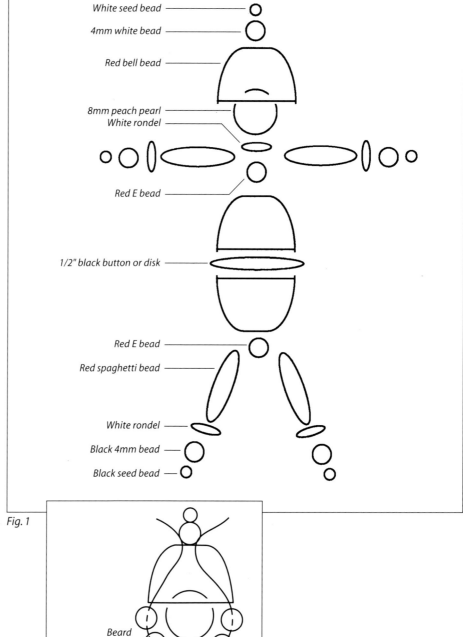

White seed bead
4mm white bead
Red bell bead
8mm peach pearl
White rondel
Red E bead
1/2" black button or disk
Red E bead
Red spaghetti bead
White rondel
Black 4mm bead
Black seed bead

Fig. 1

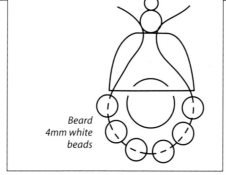

Beard
4mm white beads

Fig. 2

Pictured (from top): Bride and Groom, instructions on page 62 and 63; Santa.

Bride

Beautiful Personality

(Pictured on page 61)

Designed by Patty Cox

Finished size: 3-1/4" long

You Will Need
Supplies:
Gold wire, 28 gauge
Gold seed beads
White seed beads
Peach pearl, 8mm
Clear faceted bead, 6mm
White faceted beads, 4mm
Two peach faceted beads, 4mm
Three white bell beads
White 5/16" bugle beads
Gold crimp beads (or spacer beads)
Jewelry glue

Tools:
Toothpick
Wire cutter
Needlenose pliers

Follow These Steps
1. All multifaceted characters are made basically the same way. Follow beading charts and for more details, refer to the Betty and Ben projects on pages 68 and 70 which use the same procedures.
2. Coil hair wires around toothpick. Twist white seed beads randomly onto hair and glue to secure.⟨

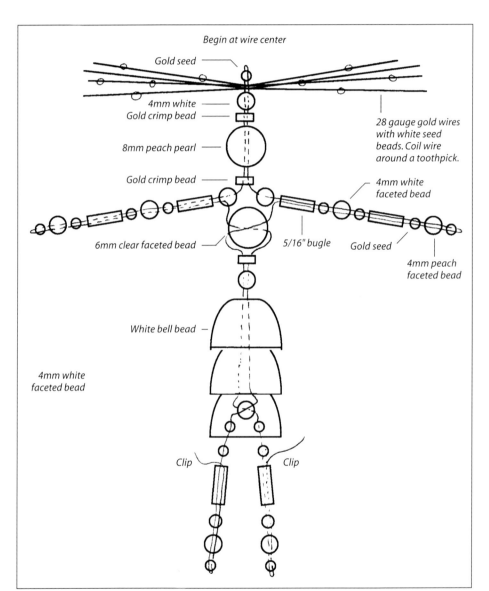

Begin at wire center

Gold seed

4mm white
Gold crimp bead

28 gauge gold wires
with white seed
beads. Coil wire
around a toothpick.

8mm peach pearl

Gold crimp bead

4mm white
faceted bead

6mm clear faceted bead

5/16" bugle

Gold seed

4mm peach
faceted bead

White bell bead

4mm white
faceted bead

Clip   Clip

Fig. 1

Groom
Handsome Personality
Pictured on page 61)

Designed by Patty Cox

Finished size: 3" long

You Will Need

Supplies:
Gold wire, 28 gauge
Gold seed beads
Black seed beads
Peach pearl, 8mm
Two peach faceted beads, 4mm
Three black faceted beads, 6mm
Black faceted beads, 4mm
Black 3/8" bugle beads
Black button or disk, 1/2" (14mm) diam.

Tools:
Toothpick
Wire cutter
Needlenose pliers

Follow These Steps
All multifaceted characters are made basically the same way. Follow beading charts and for more details, refer to the Betty and Ben projects on pages 68 and 70 which use the same procedures.◖

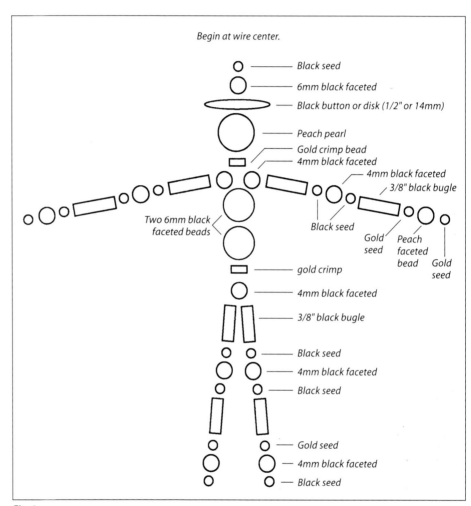

Begin at wire center.

Black seed

6mm black faceted

Black button or disk (1/2" or 14mm)

Peach pearl

Gold crimp bead

4mm black faceted

4mm black faceted

3/8" black bugle

Two 6mm black faceted beads

Black seed

Gold seed

Peach faceted bead

Gold seed

gold crimp

4mm black faceted

3/8" black bugle

Black seed

4mm black faceted

Black seed

Gold seed

4mm black faceted

Black seed

Fig. 1

Cheerleader
Spunky Personality
(Pictured on page 65)

Designed by Patty Cox

Finished size: Approximately 3" long

You Will Need
Supplies:
Gold wire, 28 gauge
Gold seed beads
Peach pearl, 8mm
Two peach pearls, 4mm
Blue bead, 6mm
Blue faceted beads, 4mm
Two clear faceted beads, 4mm
White 5/16" bugle beads
Blue 3/16" bugle beads
Silver spacer bead
Two yellow E beads
Four blue E beads
Frosted yellow bell bead
Gold scrubby pad
Bridal tulle in school colors, 1" x 18" each
    color

Tools:
Wire cutter
Needlenose pliers

Follow These Steps
1. All multifaceted characters are made basically the same way. Follow beading charts and for more details, refer to the Betty and Ben projects on pages 68 and 70 which use the same procedures.
2. Pompons: Gather down center of length of each tulle strip with your fingers. (Fig. 2.) Wrap gathers with wire. *(Fig. 3)*
3. Wire a pompon tightly around each hand bead.◖

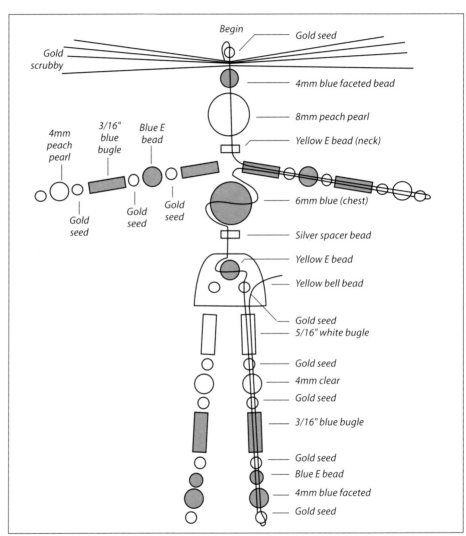

Begin — Gold seed
Gold scrubby
4mm blue faceted bead
8mm peach pearl
Yellow E bead (neck)
4mm peach pearl
3/16" blue bugle
Blue E bead
Gold seed
Gold seed
Gold seed
6mm blue (chest)
Silver spacer bead
Yellow E bead
Yellow bell bead
Gold seed
5/16" white bugle
Gold seed
4mm clear
Gold seed
3/16" blue bugle
Gold seed
Blue E bead
4mm blue faceted
Gold seed

Fig. 1

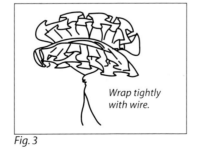

Wrap tightly with wire.

Fig. 3

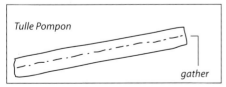

Tulle Pompon

gather

Fig. 2

Pictured (clockwise from top left): Soccer Girl & Boy, instructions on page 67; Cheerleader, instructions on page 64; Teen Girl & Boy, instructions on page 66.

Teen Girl
Sunny Personality
(Pictured on page 65)

Designed by Patty Cox

Finished Length: Approximately 3"

You Will Need

Supplies:
Gold wire, 28 gauge
Gold seed beads
Peach pearl, 8mm
Purple faceted bead, 6mm
Purple faceted beads, 4mm
Four clear faceted beads, 4mm
Gold crimp beads or spacer beads
White 3/16" bugle beads
Clear frosted bell bead
Gold scrubby pad

Tools:
Wire cutter
Needlenose pliers

Follow These Steps
All multifaceted characters are made basically the same way. Follow beading charts and for more details, refer to the Betty and Ben projects on pages 68 and 70 which use the same procedures.◖

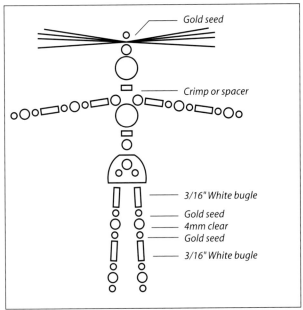

Fig. 1

Teen Boy
Adventurous Personality
(Pictured on page 65)

Designed by Patty Cox

Finished Length: Approximately 3"

You Will Need

Supplies:
Gold wire, 28 gauge
Gold seed beads
Peach pearl, 8mm
Clear faceted bead, 6mm
Four clear faceted beads, 4mm
Purple faceted beads, 4mm
White 3/16" bugle beads
Purple 3/16" bugle beads
Gold crimp beads or spacer beads
Gold scrubby pad

Tools:
Wire cutter
Needlenose pliers

Follow These Steps
All multifaceted characters are made basically the same way. Follow beading charts and for more details, refer to the Betty and Ben projects on pages 68 and 70 which use the same procedures.◖

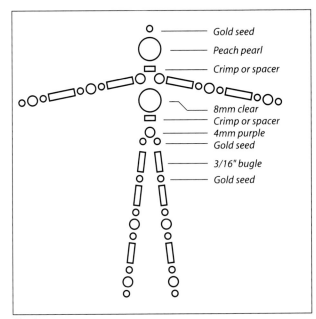

Fig. 1

Soccer Girl & Soccer Boy

Energetic Personalities

(Pictured on page 65)

Designed by Patty Cox

Finished Length: Approximately 3"

For Soccer Girl, You Will Need

Supplies:
Gold wire, 28 gauge
Seed beads: gold, black, and white
Peach pearl, 8mm
Black faceted bead, 6mm
Black faceted beads, 4mm
Clear faceted bead, 4mm
Two peach pearls, 4mm
White 5/16" bugle beads
Two white bell beads
Gold crimp bead or spacer beads
Gold scrubby pad

Tools:
Wire cutter
Needlenose pliers

For Soccer Boy, You Will Need

Supplies:
Gold wire, 28 gauge
Seed beads: gold, black, and white
Peach pearl, 8mm
Black faceted bead, 6mm
Black faceted beads, 4mm
Clear faceted bead, 4mm
Two peach pearls, 4mm
White 5/16" bugle beads
Black bell bead
White rondel bead
Gold crimp beads or spacer beads
Gold scrubby pad

Tools:
Wire cutter
Needlenose pliers

Follow These Steps

All multifaceted characters are made basically the same way. Follow beading charts and for more details, refer to the Betty and Ben projects on pages 68 and 70 which use the same procedures. Bell beads are skirt and soccer helmet. Black and white seed beads represent striped shirt.❦

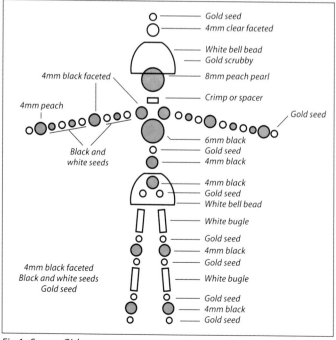

Fig 1. Soccer Girl

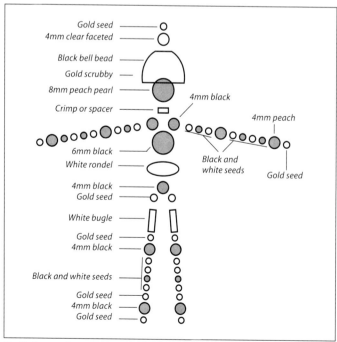

Fig 2. Soccer Boy

Ben and Betty

Winning Personalities

(Pictured on page 69)

Designed by Patty Cox

Directions for Betty

Finished Length: Approximately 3"

You Will Need

Supplies:
Gold wire, 28 gauge
Gold seed beads
Peach pearl, 8mm
Brown faceted bead, 6mm
Brown faceted beads, 4mm
Four clear faceted beads, 4mm
White 5/16" bugle beads
Gold crimp beads or spacer beads
Clear frosted bell bead

Tools:
Toothpick
Wire cutter
Needlenose pliers

Follow These Steps

Make the Head and Neck:

1. Cut a 36" length of 28 gauge gold wire. Thread a gold seed bead on center of wire and fold wire over bead. This will be top.
2. Cut four 6" lengths of gold wire. Hold between the two wires from seed beads. These will later make hair. Continue bead sequence. Thread a 4mm brown bead on both wires. Thread an 8mm peach pearl then a gold crimp bead or spacer bead on both wires. Pull wires tightly. (Follow the beading diagram in Fig. 1, as you bead the figure.

Make the Arms:

1. Separate wires from last bead. On one wire, thread a 4mm brown bead, a white bugle bead, a gold seed bead, 4mm clear faceted bead, gold seed bead, white bugle bead, gold seed bead, 4mm brown bead, and a gold seed bead. Bring wire around last

seed bead, then thread wire back through all the beads of arm, returning to below neck.
2. Repeat the procedure and sequence on other wire for other arm.

Make the Body:

1. Add a 6mm brown bead on one wire. Run the other wire through the same bead from the opposite direction. On both wires as one, thread a gold crimp or spacer bead, a 4mm brown bead, and the bell bead.
2. Under bell bead, thread one wire through a 4mm brown bead. Thread other wire through same bead from the opposite direction. Pull wires tightly.

Make the Legs:

1. On one wire, thread a gold seed bead, a bugle bead, gold seed bead, 4mm clear bead, fold seed bead, bugle bead, gold seed bead, 4mm brown bead, and a gold seed bead. Bring wire around last seed bead, then thread wire back through all beads of leg.
2. Repeat step one on other wire for other leg.
3. Clip excess wire.

Hair:
Coil each hair wire around a toothpick for a total of six curls.◖

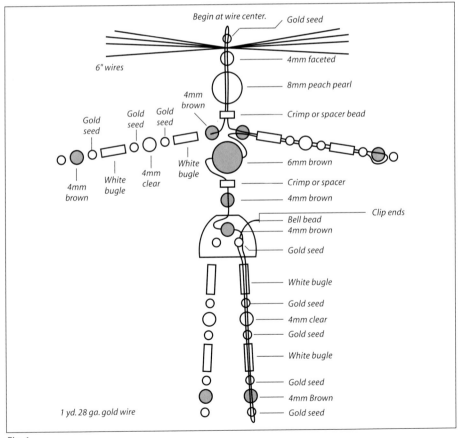

Fig. 1

Pictured (from top): Ben and Betty, instructions on pages 68 and 70; Baby Girl and Boy, instructions on pages 71 and 72

Ben and Betty

Winning Personalities

(Pictured on page 69)

Designed by Patty Cox

Directions for Ben

Finished Length: Approximately 2-3/4"

You Will Need

Supplies:
Gold wire, 28 gauge
Gold seed beads
Peach pearl, 8mm
Brown faceted bead, 8mm
Brown faceted beads, 4mm
Two peach faceted beads, 4mm
Brown 3/16" bugle beads
Gold crimp beads or spacer beads

Tools:
Toothpick
Wire cutter
Needlenose pliers

Follow These Steps

Make the Head and Neck:

1. Cut a 36" length of 28 gauge gold wire. Thread a gold seed bead on center of wire and fold wire over bead. This will be top.
2. Cut two 4" lengths of gold wire. Hold between the two wires from seed beads. These will later make hair. Continue bead sequence. Thread a 4mm brown bead on both wires. Thread an 8mm peach pearl then a gold crimp bead or spacer bead on both wires. Pull wires tightly. (Follow the beading diagram in Fig. 1, as you bead the figure.)

Make the Arms:

1. Separate wires from last bead. On one wire, thread a 4mm brown bead, a brown bugle bead, gold seed bead, 4mm brown faceted bead, gold seed bead, brown bugle bead, gold seed bead, 4mm peach bead, and a gold seed bead. Bring wire around last

seed bead, then thread wire back through all the beads of arm, returning to below neck.
2. Repeat the procedure and sequence on other wire for other arm.

Make the Body:

1. Add an 8mm brown bead on one wire. Run the other wire through the same bead from the opposite direction. On both wires as one, thread a gold crimp or spacer bead.
2. Thread one wire through a 4mm brown bead. Thread other wire through same bead from the opposite direction. Pull wires tightly.

Make the Legs:

1. On one wire, thread a gold seed bead, a bugle bead, gold seed bead, a bugle bead, gold seed bead, 4mm brown bead, gold seed bead, bugle bead, gold seed bead, 4mm brown bead, and a gold seed bead. Bring wire around last seed bead, then thread wire back through all beads of leg.
2. Repeat step one on other wire for other leg.
3. Clip excess wire.

Hair:

Coil each hair wire around a toothpick to make curls.⟪

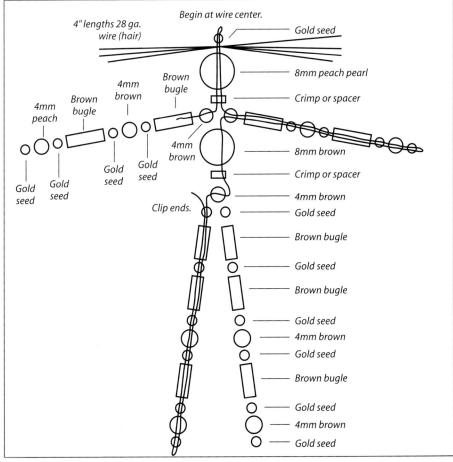

Fig 1.

Baby Girl
Innocent Personalities
(Pictured on page 69)

Designed by Patty Cox

Finished Length: 1-1/2"

You Will Need
Supplies:
Gold wire, 28 gauge
Gold seed beads
Peach pearl, 8mm
Two pink beads, 4mm
White 3/16" bugle beads
Crimp bead
White frosted bell bead

Tools:
Toothpick
Needlenose pliers

Follow These Steps
All Multifaceted characters are made basically the same way. Follow beading charts and for more details, refer to the Betty and Ben projects on pages 68 and 70 which use the same procedures. Use a single 3" gold wire for hair.❁

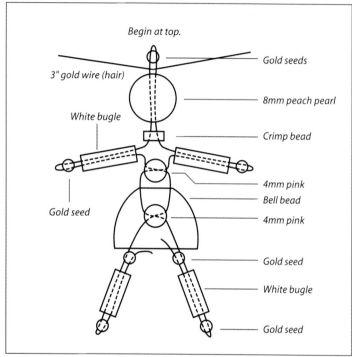

Begin at top.

3" gold wire (hair)

White bugle

Gold seed

Gold seeds

8mm peach pearl

Crimp bead

4mm pink
Bell bead
4mm pink

Gold seed

White bugle

Gold seed

Fig 1.

Baby Boy

Innocent Personalities

(Pictured on page 69)

Designed by Patty Cox

Finished Length: 1-1/2"

You Will Need

Supplies:
Gold wire, 28 gauge
Gold seed beads
Peach pearl, 8mm
Gold crimp bead
Blue faceted bead, 4mm
Blue faceted bead, 6mm
White 3/16" bugle beads

Tools:
Toothpick
Needlenose pliers

Follow These Steps

All Multifaceted characters are made basically the same way. Follow beading charts that show wire paths. *(Fig. 1)* (For more details, refer to the Betty and Ben projects on pages 68 and 70 which use the same procedures.) Use a single 3" gold wire for hair.

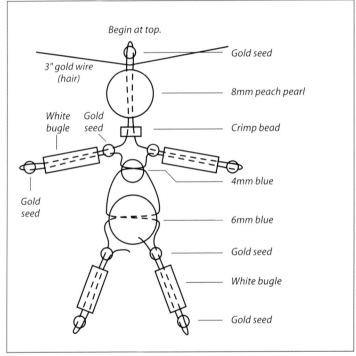

Fig 1.

Birthstone Babies
Precious Personalities
(Pictured on page 75)

Designed by Patty Cox

Finished Length of Baby: 7/8"

You Will Need
Supplies:
Gold wire, 28 gauge
Gold seed beads
Gold bead, 3mm
Two 4mm faceted beads in selected birthstone color

Tools:
Needlenose pliers

Follow These Steps
All Multifaceted characters are made basically the same way. Follow beading charts that show wire paths. *(Fig. 1)* (For more details, refer to the Betty and Ben projects on pages 68 and 70 which use the same procedures.) To form a hanging loop at top, break off top seed bead with needlenose pliers after beading the entire figure, leaving a wire loop. Curve babies' legs slightly outward—"bow" them.❝

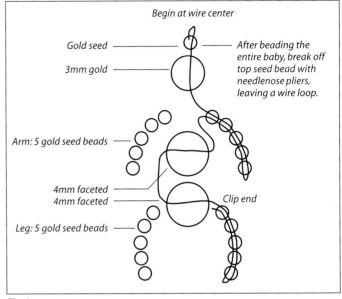

Begin at wire center

Gold seed

3mm gold

After beading the entire baby, break off top seed bead with needlenose pliers, leaving a wire loop.

Arm: 5 gold seed beads

4mm faceted
4mm faceted

Clip end

Leg: 5 gold seed beads

Fig. 1

Necklace
Finished Length: 24"

You Will Need
Supplies:
Birthstone Babies (see previous instructions), as many as desired in colors desired
Necklace chain, 24"
Gold eyepins, enough to go between and on each side of babies
Gold jump rings

Tools:
Round nose pliers
Needlenose pliers

Follow These Steps
1. Bend gold eyepins into coils and/or square coils, using needlenose or round nose pliers. (Figs. 2 and 3)
2. Attach birthstone babies on necklace chain with jump rings.
3. Attach eyepin coils between and on each end of birthstone babies.❝

Fashion Pin
Finished Width: 2-3/4"

You Will Need
Supplies:
Birthstone Babies (see instructions), as many as desired in colors desired
Gold wire, 28 gauge
Gold skirt pin

Tools:
Round nose pliers
Needlenose pliers

Follow These Steps
1. Cut one yard of 28 gauge gold wire.
2. Tightly wrap wire around closed end of pin, wrapping through loop of babies as you wrap, attaching them to pin. *(Fig. 4)* ❝

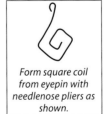

Form square coil from eyepin with needlenose pliers as shown.

Fig. 2

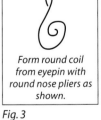

Form round coil from eyepin with round nose pliers as shown.

Fig. 3

Fig. 4

Birthstone Buddies Earrings
Treasured Personalities
(Pictured on page 75)

Designed by Patty Cox

Finished Length of Earring (excluding findings): 1"

You Will Need
Supplies:
Gold wire, 28 gauge
Gold seed beads
Gold bead, 3mm
Two 4mm faceted beads in selected birthstone color
Set of gold fish hook earwires

Tools:
Needlenose pliers

All Multifaceted characters are made basically the same way. Follow beading charts that show wire paths. *(Fig. 1)* (For more details, refer to the Betty and Ben projects on pages 68 and 70 which use the same procedures.) To form a hanging loop at top, break off top seed bead with needlenose pliers after beading the entire figure, leaving a wire loop.❧

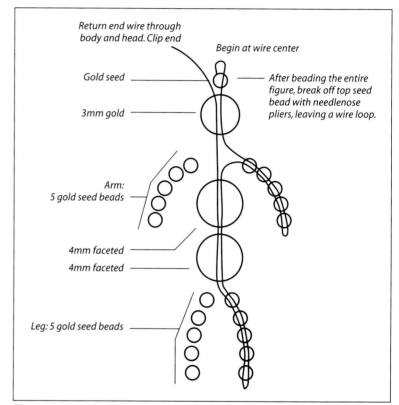

Return end wire through body and head. Clip end

Begin at wire center

Gold seed

After beading the entire figure, break off top seed bead with needlenose pliers, leaving a wire loop.

3mm gold

Arm:
5 gold seed beads

4mm faceted
4mm faceted

Leg: 5 gold seed beads

Fig 1.

Pictured: Birthstone Babies Necklace & Pin, instructions on page 73; Birthstone Buddies Earrings, instructions on page 74

Wire Mesh Jewelry

Who would believe it's wire! Yes, it's wire woven like mesh (fewer and larger wires per inch) or like fabric (many and finer wires per inch). It even feels like fabric, but has that special sheen of metal. And the best part is that it can often be used like fabric.

Cover buttons. Make a little purse. The jewelry in this section does just that, combining the cloth designs with wired beads and wire spirals and coils and other artistic combinations.

Amaze yourself (and your friends) with a wire cloth jewelry creation!

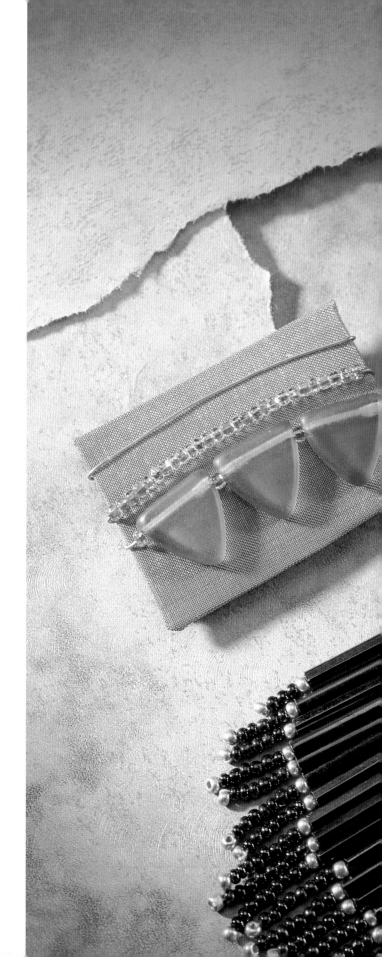

Beaded Purse
Pendant

Designed by Patty Cox

Finished Length of Necklace: 22" plus pendant

You Will Need

Supplies:
Bronze wire mesh, 40 gauge: 3-3/4" x 2" piece
Gold wire, 24 gauge
Gold seed beads
Purple/blue seed beads
Purple/blue 1" bugle beads
Beading thread

Tools:
Beading needle
T-pin
Needlenose pliers

Follow These Steps

Make the Wire Mesh Purse:
1. Cut wire mesh to 3-3/4" x 2" according to pattern given. Fold top long edge to back. Crimp folded edge with needlenose pliers to form 1/8" hem.
2. Fold purse sides to back. Fold lines are indicated on pattern.
3. Coil 24 gauge gold wire to a 3-1/4" length. (See "How to Coil Wire With a Drill" in General Instructions.) Loop the coil and position it on purse front as shown in photo of project. Insert wire ends of coil through the wire mesh and press them flat. (The holes in mesh where you push the wire ends through may need to be enlarged by pushing a T-pin into mesh.)
4. Fold raw edges of mesh together on backside 1/8". Fold again. (Fig. 1)

Make the Beaded Purse Fringe:
1. Thread beading needle with beading thread. Insert needle through mesh at side bottom of purse, leaving a thread tail. Follow the beading chart as you add the beads. Begin where shown in Fig. 2. Add

top seed beads, bugle beads, and bottom seed beads. Go through and around last gold seed bead and return through all beads to top. Bring needle through both layers of purse bottom and start the next strand of fringe. Repeat the same procedure all the way across purse bottom. Strands will increase in length to center, then decrease in length to other side.
2. To finish, insert needle (from last strand of fringe) through inside of purse bottom and exit near beginning tail thread. Tie threads into a knot and clip ends. Push

knot to inside of purse, using a T-pin.

Make the Beaded Necklace:
1. Cut a 24" length of beading thread. Knot one end. Insert needle from inside upper corner of purse. Thread on beads according to Fig. 3, repeating the sequence shown in the diagram twelve more times, then ending with the seed beads at the beginning of the sequence.
2. End thread inside purse on other upper corner. Tie knot. Clip ends.❝

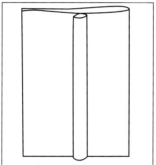

Fig. 1

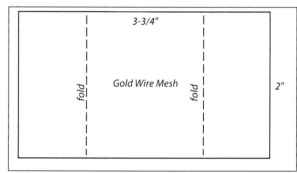

Pattern for Purse

3-3/4"

fold *Gold Wire Mesh* *fold* *2"*

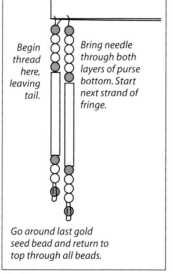

Begin thread here, leaving tail.

Bring needle through both layers of purse bottom. Start next strand of fringe.

Go around last gold seed bead and return to top through all beads.

Fig. 2

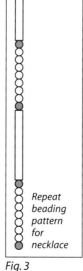

Repeat beading pattern for necklace

Fig. 3

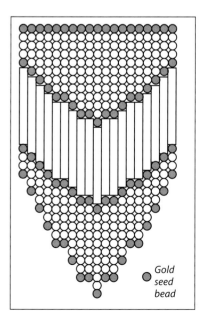

● *Gold seed bead*

Beading Diagram

Gold and Copper
Covered Button Earrings
(Pictured on page 81)

Designed by Patty Cox

Finished Size of Earring: 1" diam.

You Will Need
Supplies:
Two 2" circles gold wire mesh cloth, 100 gauge
Brown or antique copper wire, 24 gauge
Two 1" button blanks for covered buttons
Post or clip earring backs
Jewelry glue

Tools:
Nylon jaw pliers
Needlenose pliers

Follow These Steps
1. Cut two 2" circles from wire cloth (pattern given).
2. Fold edges of a wire cloth circle over sides of button blank onto clawtooth back. Press mesh around button with thumbs, pressing out creases and puckers.
3. Turn button over. Use the end of needlenose pliers to force wire cloth tightly under clawtooth.
4. Coil two 3-1/4" coiled lengths of brown (antique copper) wire. Form a loop with coil as shown. *Fig. 2.* Position on button as shown and bend ending wires from coil over edges of button to backside.
5. Position covered button backer over wire cloth and wire coil ends. Press backer, locking it into the button. Carefully use nylon jaw pliers to secure button front to back, being careful not to dent button front.
6. Glue earring posts on button backs.⟨

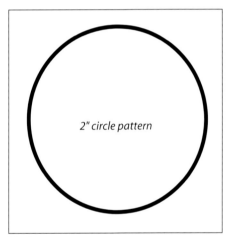

2" circle pattern

Fig. 1

Fig. 2

Pictured (from top:) Gold and Copper Earrings, instructions on page 80; Gold Cloth With Spiral Pin, instructions on page 82; Gold Cloth with Czech Beads Pin, instructions on page 83

Gold Cloth with Spiral
Fashion Pin
(Pictured on page 81)

Designed by Caren Carr

Finished Size of Pin: 1-1/8" (30mm) square

You Will Need
Supplies:
Aluminum wire, 17 gauge
Copper wire, 24 gauge
Gold wire mesh, 100 gauge
White cardboard
Small piece ultrasuede or leather
Electrical tape
Adhesive for leather
Pin back, 1"

Tools:
Round nose pliers
Wire cutters
Flat nose pliers
Scissors suitable for cutting gold wire mesh
File

Follow These Steps
Make Gold Mesh Square:
1. Cut cardboard to a 30mm square.
2. Cut a piece of gold mesh larger than cardboard—large enough to wrap around edges.
3. With flat nose pliers, crimp gold mesh around edges of cardboard, mitering corners.

Make Flat Coil:
1. Cut a 12" length of 17 gauge wire. File the ends.
2. Using round nose pliers, spiral wire into a tight flat coil. As you reach outside edges, you may need to use fingers only, in order to keep the spiral on the same plane. Cut off remaining 1-1/2" of wire. End of spiral should gently curve into itself. *(Fig. 1)*

Assemble Pin:
1. Place flat coil in center of mesh square.

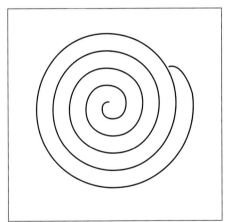

Fig. 1

2. Cut four 4" lengths of copper wire.
3. Insert a copper wire into outside curve of flat coil and pull it tightly around the aluminum wire of coil. Center of copper wire will be around aluminum wire. Twist the two ends of the copper wire tightly for a distance of 3/8". Repeat with remaining copper wires at the other three directional points around flat coil. *(Fig. 2)*
3. Bring twisted wires around square on each edge and twist opposite sets of wires tightly together on backside (two sets of twists). Cut off excess and secure with a small piece of electrical tape.
4. Cut a small piece of ultrasuede or leather to cover wires and raw edges of gold mesh on backside. Glue in place. Let dry.
5. Glue pin back on back of square.☙

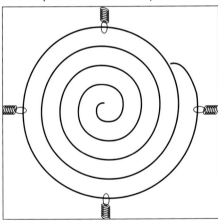

Fig. 2

Gold Cloth with Czech Beads

Fashion Pin

(Pictured on page 81)

Designed by Caren Carr

Finished Size of Pin: 1-5/8" x 1-1/8"
(40mm x 30mm)

You Will Need

Supplies:

Gold wire mesh, 100 gauge
Copper wire, 24 gauge
Blue cardboard
Three blue Czech glass flat beads
Gold translucent seed beads
Small piece ultrasuede or leather
Electrical tape
Adhesive for leather
Pin back, 1"

Tools:

Wire cutters
Flat nose pliers
Scissors suitable for cutting gold mesh
File

Follow These Steps

Make Gold Mesh Rectangle:

1. Cut a piece of cardboard to 40mm x 30mm.
2. Cut a piece of gold mesh larger than cardboard with enough to wrap around edges.
3. With flat nose pliers, crimp gold mesh around edges of cardboard, mitering corners.

Beads and Wire:

1. String onto wire: Gold seed bead, Czech bead, gold seed bead, Czech bead, gold seed bead, Czech bead, and gold seed bead. (Fig. 1)
2. Wrap this tightly onto covered cardboard base and twist wires in back to secure. The beads cross the front of mesh base with the natural curve (sad face) of the wire rather than straight across.
3. On wire, string gold translucent seed beads for the width of the mesh base. Repeat step 2 above as the Czech beads. Make sure that there are no seed beads on the edges of the pin—they should all be on the front.
4. Repeat step 2 with a piece of copper wire.
5. Cut off excess wire.
6. Check the front of the pin and adjust placement of wires, if needed, to achieve the curving parallel lines.

Assemble Pin:

1. Secure wires on backside with a small piece of electrical tape.
2. Cut a small piece of ultrasuede or leather to cover wires and raw edges of gold mesh on backside. Glue in place. Let dry.
3. Glue pin back on back of square.⸫

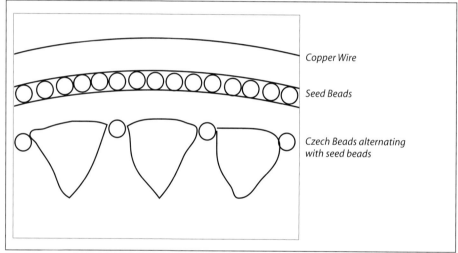

Fig. 1

Copper Wire

Seed Beads

Czech Beads alternating with seed beads

Wire Wild Critters

The attraction to nature in artistic pursuits is very strong today, perhaps to balance our high-tech, urban, 21st century world. These jewelry pieces capture nature's magic and add a touch of Earth in a beautiful sparkly or shiny manner.

Picture dragonflies made of glittering beads strung on wire ... butterflies made of metal cloth ... or a spider of twisted and coiled copper. If you have any trouble picturing these, just turn the next few pages and see the photos for yourself. Then follow the easy instructions to make a few. Enrich your accessory wardrobe and your soul.

Dragonfly with Glass Wings
Fashion Pin
(Pictured on page 87)

Designed by Patty Cox

Finished Length of Pin: 4-1/4"

You Will Need
Supplies:
Gold wire, 24 gauge
Gold wire, 28 gauge
Seven gold seed beads
Four turquoise teardrop glass beads,
 3/4" long
Three gold crimp beads
Blue glass bead, 8mm
Green glass bead, 7mm
Two blue glass beads, 6mm
Turquoise diamond glass bead
Green diamond glass bead
Blue glass bead, 4mm
Green glass bead, 4mm
Pin back

Tools:
Needlenose pliers
Round nose pliers

Follow These Steps
Beaded Wings, Body & Tail:
1. Beginning with a seed bead at head, thread beads onto 24 gauge wire, following the beading diagram. *(Fig. 1)*
2. Twist ending wires together at tail. Coil twisted ending wires, using round nose pliers.
3. Break off the top seed bead with needlenose pliers, leaving a wire loop at head.

Add Antennae & Pin Back:
1. Twist together two 6" lengths of 24 gauge wire.
2. Thread twisted wires through loop at head. fold to find center. Twist antennae at head to secure them.
3. Shape each antenna as shown with round nose pliers.
4. Wire pin to backside of dragonfly with 28 gauge wire.❧

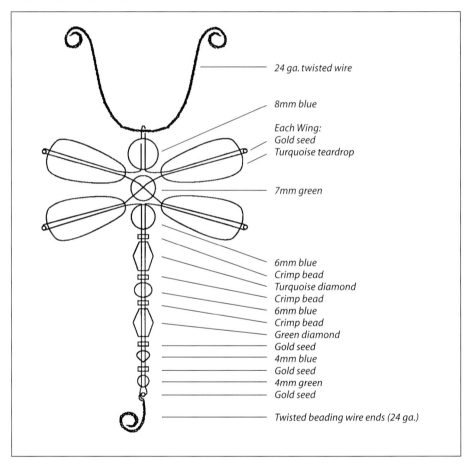

24 ga. twisted wire

8mm blue

Each Wing:
Gold seed
Turquoise teardrop

7mm green

6mm blue
Crimp bead
Turquoise diamond
Crimp bead
6mm blue
Crimp bead
Green diamond
Gold seed
4mm blue
Gold seed
4mm green
Gold seed

Twisted beading wire ends (24 ga.)

Pictured (from top left): Dragonfly with Glass Wings Pin, instructions on page 86; Iridescent Blue Dragonfly Hairpin, instructions on page 89; Dragonfly with Beaded Wings Pin, instructions on page 88

Dragonfly with Beaded Wings
Fashion Pin
(Pictured on page 87)

Designed by Patty Cox

Finished Length of Pin: 3-1/2"

You Will Need
Supplies:
Gold wire, 24 gauge
Gold wire, 32 gauge
Two gold seed beads
Green iris seed beads
Clear seed beads
Green glass bead, 8mm
Two silver spacer beads
Gold bead, 5mm
Green glass bead, 5mm
Two gold beads, 3mm
Turquoise diamond shaped glass bead,
    1/4" long
Green diamond glass bead, 5/8" long
Silver oval bead, 1/2" long
Pin back

Tools:
Needlenose pliers
Round nose pliers

Follow These Steps
Body/Tail:
1. Beginning with a gold seed bead at head, thread beads onto 24 gauge wire according to the beading diagram. *(Fig. 1)*
2. Twist ending wires together at tail. Coil twisted ending wires, using round nose pliers.

Beaded Wings:
With 32 gauge wire, weave four seed bead wings, following the beading patterns in Fig. 2 (upper wings) and Fig. 3 (lower wings).

Assemble Pin:
1. Wire each wing onto dragonfly body.
2. Wire pin back to back of dragonfly.❦

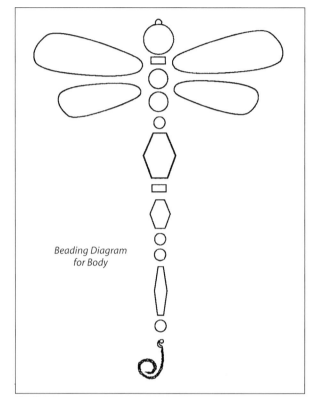

Beading Diagram for Body

Fig. 1

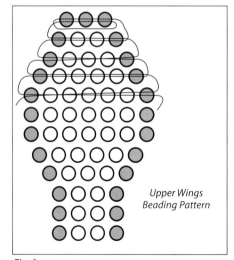

Upper Wings Beading Pattern

Fig. 2

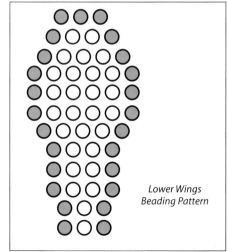

Lower Wings Beading Pattern

Fig. 3

Iridescent Blue Dragonfly
Hairpin
(Pictured on page 87)

Designed by Patty Cox

Finished Length of Pin: 2-1/2"

You Will Need
Supplies:
Gold wire, 24 gauge
Gold wire, 28 gauge: 12" length
Six gold seed beads
Blue faceted bead, 8mm
Three clear faceted beads, 6mm
Two blue faceted bead, 6mm
Blue faceted bead, 4mm
Clear faceted bead, 4mm
Four iridescent blue spaghetti beads
Hair pin

Tools:
Needlenose pliers
Round nose pliers

Follow These Steps
1. Beginning with a seed bead at head, thread beads onto 24 gauge wire as shown on beading diagram. *(Fig. 1)*
2. Twist ending wires together. Coil ending wires with round nose pliers.
3. Wire dragonfly to hair pin with 28 gauge wire.❰

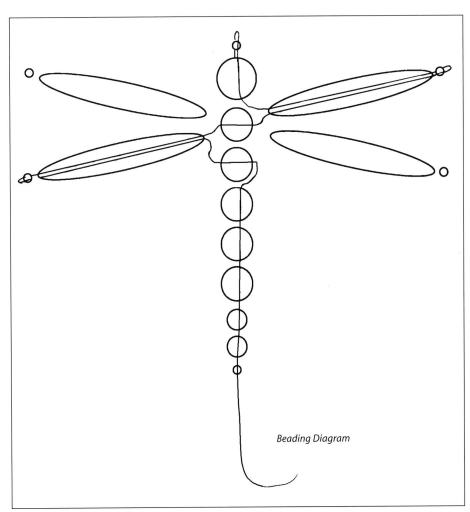

Beading Diagram

Fig. 1

Gold Butterfly
Fashion Pin
(Pictured on page 91)

Designed by Patty Cox

Finished Size of Pin: 2-1/4" x 2"

You Will Need
Supplies:
Bronze wire mesh, 40 gauge: 2" x 2-1/2" piece
Gold wire, 24 gauge
Pin back

Tools:
Power drill
Buss wire, 10" length
Round nose pliers
Needlenose pliers

Follow These Steps
Wings:
1. Cut wire mesh butterfly according to the pattern given.
2. Fold all raw edges under 1/8". Crimp edges flat with needlenose pliers. Fold and crease mesh between top and bottom wings. Fold butterfly center.
3. Lightly curve mesh to shape each wing.

Body:
1. Tightly coil 24 gauge gold wire to a 1" length for butterfly body. (See "How To Coil Wire With a Drill" in General Instructions.)
2. Wire the ends of coil around butterfly center.

Antennae:
1. Twist together two 3" lengths of 24 gauge gold wire for antennae.
2. Fold twisted wire in half. Coil each end with round nose pliers. Wire antennae to butterfly at top of body.
3. Wire pin back onto center back of butterfly.◖

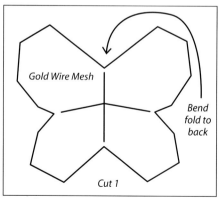
Gold Wire Mesh

Bend fold to back

Cut 1

Butterfly Pattern

Copper Spider
Fashion Pin
(Pictured on page 91)

Designed by Patty Cox

Finished Size of Pin: 1-3/4"

You Will Need
Supplies:
Copper wire, 20 gauge
Black half bead, 5mm
Pin back
Jewelry glue

Tools:
Flat coil maker (see "Constructing a Flat Coil" in General Instructions)
T-pin
Needlenose pliers

Follow These Steps
1. Form a 1/2" diameter flat coil with 20 gauge copper wire. With same wire, make six legs as shown in diagram. *(Fig. 1)* Cut wire, leaving a 6" tail. With the 6" tail, form a smaller spiral as shown.
2. To twist each leg, stick a T-pin in bent end, hold base of leg with needlenose pliers, then twist. *(Fig. 2)*
3. Bend larger body spiral over smaller head spiral. *(Fig. 3)* Bend legs as shown.
4. Glue black half bead in center of body spiral.
5. Glue pin back on underside of spider body.◖

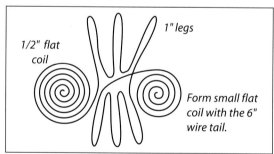
1/2" flat coil

1" legs

Form small flat coil with the 6" wire tail.

Fig. 1

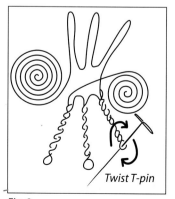
Twist T-pin

Fig. 2

Fig. 3

Pictured (clockwise from top: Coiled Bumble Bee Knots Earrings, instructions on page 93; Seed Bead Bee, instructions on page 92; Gold Butterfly pin, instructions on page 90; Copper Spider Pin, instructions on page 90

Seed Bead Bee
Hair Clip
(Pictured on page 91)

Designed by Patty Cox

Finished Size of Hair Clip: 2" (including antennae)

You Will Need
Supplies:
Gold wire, 32 gauge
Black wire, 24 gauge: 12" length
Seed beads: Yellow, black, and clear
Gold hair clip, 1" long

Tools:
Toothpick
Needlenose pliers

Follow These Steps
Bee Body:
1. Cut a 28" length of 32 gauge gold wire. Beginning at top of bee, thread six black beads to center of wire. Bring end of wire around beads to other side and run it back through beads. *(Fig. 1)* Pull wires tightly.
2. Thread seven yellow beads on wire. Run end of wire through beads in the opposite direction. *(Fig. 2)* Pull wires tightly.
3. Continue threading beads on each row, following the Beading Chart *(Fig. 3)*.
4. Run beading wire ends back through previous rows of beads to secure. Clip wire ends.

Wings:
1. Cut a 24" length of 32 gauge gold wire.
2. Thread the wire through the second (yellow) row of beads from top of body. Fold wire so that center is at bee body. Thread 11 clear seed beads on wire. Form a loop, then thread the wire through the third (black) row of body beads.
3. Thread 11 more clear seed beads on wire. Thread wire back through second (yellow) row of body beads. Secure wire end by running wire through top (black) row of body beds.
4. Repeat steps 1-3 on other side of bee body for second set of wings.

Antennae & Hair Clip:
1. Cut a 12" length of 24 gauge black wire. Fold in half to find center.
2. Wrap each wire end around a toothpick to coil it irregularly.
3. Wire antennae to widest end of hair clip.
4. Secure bee body to hair clip with 32 gauge wire. *(Fig. 4)*

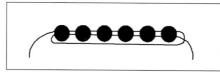

Fig. 1

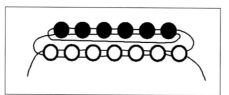

Fig. 2

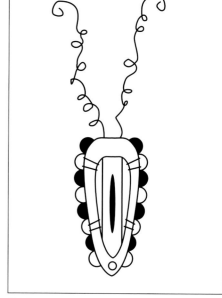

Fig. 4

Beading Chart

Thread 11 clear beads on each wing wire.

● Black
○ Yellow
◉ Clear

Fig. 3

Coiled Bumble Bee Knots
Earrings
(Pictured on page 91)

Designed by Patty Cox

Finished Length of Earring (excluding finding): 3/4"

You Will Need
Supplies:
Black wire, 24 gauge
Yellow wire, 24 gauge
Silver wire, 32 gauge
Clear seed beads
Two silver eyepins
Set of silver fish hook earring findings

Tools:
Power drill
Buss wire, 16 gauge, 10" length
Needlenose pliers

Follow These Steps
Make the Coils:
1. Insert 10" piece of buss wire and end of 24 gauge yellow wire into drill. Coil the wire to a 6" length, following instructions in "How To Coil Wire With a Drill" in General Instructions. Remove coil from wire length.
2. Make a 6" coil with 24 gauge black wire in the same manner.

Make the Bumble Bees:
1. Cut the yellow coil and the black coil in half for two 3" coils of each color. (Fig. 1)
2. Twist the wire ends of a 3" yellow coil and a 3" black coil together. (Fig. 2)
3. Wrap both coils together around a pencil. (Fig. 3)
4. Remove coils from pencil. Insert coil ends through coils, forming a knot. (Fig. 4) Gently pull ends to tighten knot. Trim wire ends.
5. Repeat steps 2-4 for second earring.

Wings & Earwires:
1. Weave four bee wings with clear seed beads and 32 gauge wire. (Fig. 5)
2. Insert the wire ends through bee body to bottom of body. (Fig. 6) Tuck twisted ends up into bee body.
3. Insert an eyepin through the top of bee. Form a hook in the eyepin below body. Press hooked end into body. (Fig. 7) Repeat with another eyepin and other bee body.
4. Attach fish hook earwires to top loops of eyepins.◖

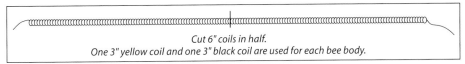

Cut 6" coils in half.
One 3" yellow coil and one 3" black coil are used for each bee body.

Fig. 1

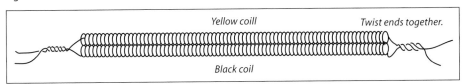

Yellow coill   Twist ends together.

Black coil

Fig. 2

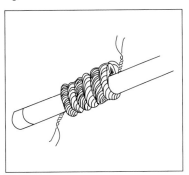

Form an overhand knot.

Trim away ends.

Fig. 3

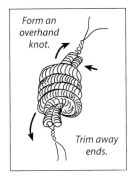

Fig. 4

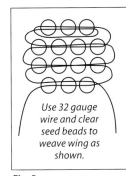

Use 32 gauge wire and clear seed beads to weave wing as shown.

Fig. 5

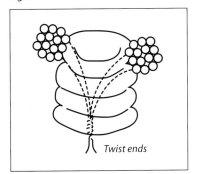

Twist ends

Fig. 6

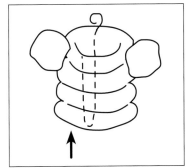

Fig. 7

Whimsical Wire Shapes

Bend wire into a favorite word (yes, a *word*) for a fashion pin. Or let your imagination soar as you create beaded wire snowflakes or contemporary curves and coils to accessorize your outfits. That's the great thing about wire—it bends to any shape! And it's beautiful with beads on it or without them.

Whimsy is welcome in this category of designs...drops, hoops, dangles, elaborate chain links, and even hammered wire designs.

If it's a unique handmade piece you want—whether for yourself or a gift—look through these pages for an exciting selection.

Believe
Stickpin

Designed by Patty Cox

Finished Width of Pin: 3-1/2"

You Will Need
Supplies:
Copper wire, 18 gauge
Copper wire, 24 gauge: 6" length
Austrian crystal bead, 3/8"

Tools:
Round nose pliers
Needlenose pliers
Nylon jaw pliers
File

Follow These Steps
1. Refer to pattern. Beginning at the small loop of the "B", slowly form letters by wrapping wire around round nose pliers.
2. Form the "i" by folding wire, then pressing together with nylon jaw pliers.
3. Finish ending the "e" by looping wire around round nose of pliers. Clip wire end.
4. Fold the center of a 6" length of 24 gauge wire through the top of the "i". Thread the crystal bead over both wires. Press bead tightly against the top of the "i". Fold wire ends over top of the bead.
5. Clip one wire, leaving the other as a stickpin. Sharpen end of stickpin wire with a file.◖

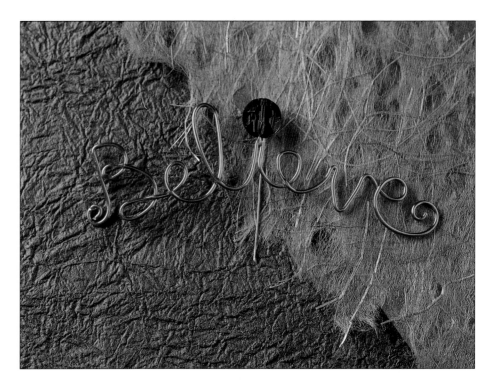

Pictured at right:
Copper and Green
Beads, instructions
on next page.

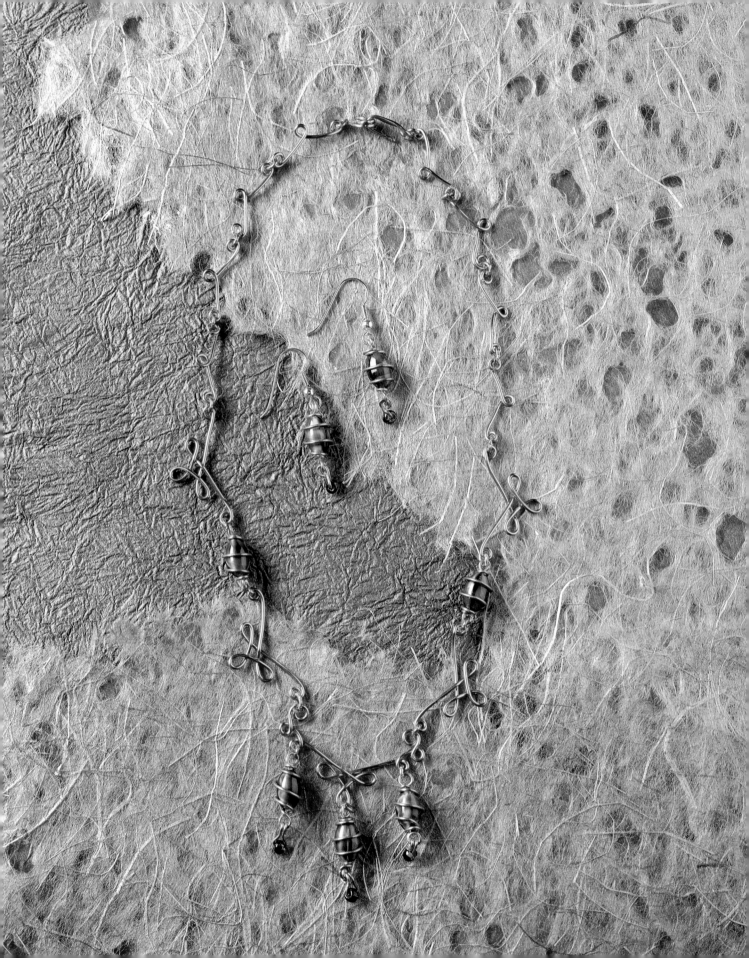

Copper and Green Beads
Necklace and Earrings

Designed by Patty Cox

Finished Length of Necklace: 16"
Finished Length of Earrings (excluding
    findings): 1"

You Will Need
Supplies:
Copper wire, 18 gauge
Seven green oval glass beads, 3/8"
Five green glass beads, 3mm
Set of fish hook earring findings

Tools:
Wire curving jig
Round nose pliers
Needlenose pliers
Nylon jaw pliers

Follow These Steps
Make Wire Links:
1. Place pegs in jig according to diagram—*Jig Diagram for Center Motif.*
2. For necklace center design cut a 12" length of copper wire. Hold one end on jig near starting peg. Begin wrapping wire around pegs according to the Jig Diagram.
3. Lift wire from jig. Trim end wires to 5/8". Form a loop on each end with round nose pliers. *(Fig. 1)*
4. Press design flat with nylon jaw pliers.
5. Make four chain sections like center design, omitting outer loops. Trim wire ends to 5/8". Form a loop on each end with round nose pliers. *(Fig. 2)* Press design flat with nylon jaw pliers.
6. Place the pegs on jig according to diagram—*Jig Diagram for Chain.*

Instructions continued on page 99

Center Design
Make 1

Fig. 1

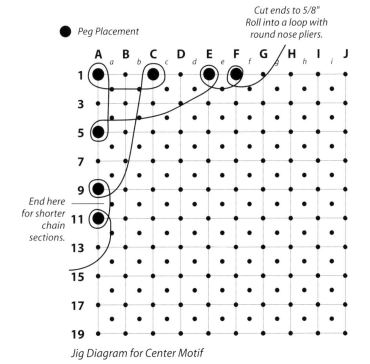

● *Peg Placement*

Cut ends to 5/8"
Roll into a loop with
round nose pliers.

*End here
for shorter
chain
sections.*

Jig Diagram for Center Motif

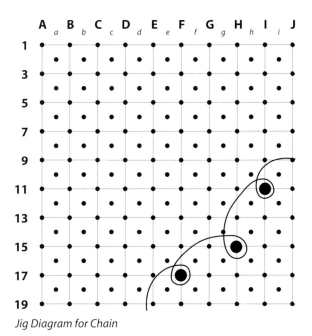

Jig Diagram for Chain

7. Make eight chain sections according to Jig Diagram.
8. Trim wire ends and form loops. *(Fig. 3)* Press designs flat.

Wrap the Beads:

1. Cut a 12" length of wire. Hold wire 1/2" from end with round nose pliers. Fold wire over round nose to form a loop. Add a green oval bead over both wires. *(Fig. 4)* Form a wire loop on other end of bead. Wrap wire tightly around loop. Wrap wire spirally around bead. Wrap wire tightly around other loop. Clip wire end as needed.
2. Repeat step 1 until you have five bead units for necklace and two for earrings (seven total).
3. Wire a dark green bead onto one loop of three oval bead units.

Make Jump Rings:

1. Hold wire in jaws of round nose pliers. Wrap wire around one rounded jaw, overlapping end. Remove wire.
2. Trim ends evenly into a circle.

Make Hook & Eye Necklace Clasp:

1. *For Hook:* Cut a 4" length of wire. Fold in half. *(Fig. 5)* Press fold together with nylon jaw pliers. Bend folded end over into a hook, using round nose pliers. *(Fig. 6)* Trim one wire end. Form other wire end into a loop.
2. *For Eye:* Cut a 4" length of wire. Form a large double ring with round nose pliers. *(Fig. 7)* Bend a smaller loop near ring. Clip excess wire end.

Assemble the Necklace & Earrings:

1. Connect all necklace chain sections with jump rings. Refer to photo of project for placement. There is a chain section similar to center design on each side of center design, then an oval bead unit (without extra bead) on each side of necklace, then another chain section similar to center on each side. From this point to ends on each side, use the eight smaller chain sections—four on each side. Connect hook to one end of necklace and eye to other end of necklace with jump rings. Connect the three dangling bead units (those with an extra bead) to the center design of necklace with jump rings.
2. Attach remaining bead units to fish hook earwires with jump rings. ⸙

Chain Section Make 4

Fig. 2

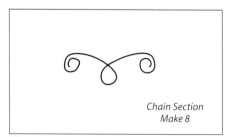

Chain Section Make 8

Fig. 3

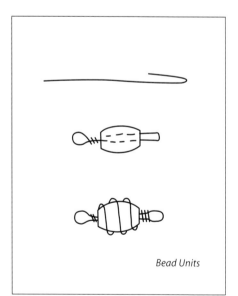

Bead Units

Fig. 4

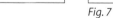

Fold

Fig. 5

Hook

Fig. 6

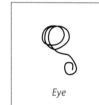

Eye

Fig. 7

Red Roses
Earrings

Designed by Patty Cox

You Will Need
Supplies:
Red wire, 22 gauge
Silver wire, 32 gauge
Green seed beads
Set of fish hook earring findings

Tools:
Round nose pliers
Needlenose pliers
Nylon jaw pliers

Follow These Steps
Form Roses:
1. Beginning at rose center, wrap red wire around round nose pliers, forming a circle.

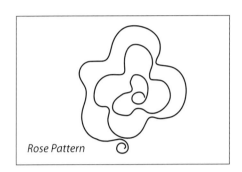

Rose Pattern

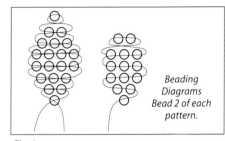

Beading Diagrams Bead 2 of each pattern.

Fig. 1

2. Form a wire petal, following pattern given. Hold end of petal to center circle with round nose pliers, then form next petal. Continue adding petals.
3. End rose by forming an ending loop. Clip wire.
4. Repeat steps 1-3 for second rose.

Leaves & Earwires:
1. Weave four green seed bead leaves—two for each rose—following beading diagrams. *(Fig. 1)*
2. Wire leaves to ending loop on rose for each earring.
3. Attach fish hook earwires around a top petal of each rose.◖

Green Figure Eights
Earrings

Designed by Patty Cox

You Will Need
Supplies:
Dark green wire, 24 gauge
Gold wire, 32 gauge
Set of silver fish hook earring findings

Tools:
Wire-curving jig
Round nose pliers
Needlenose pliers
Nylon jaw pliers

Follow These Steps
1. Place pegs in jig according to Fig. 1.
2. Cut an 18" length of dark green wire. Hold one end on top corner of jig. Begin wrapping wire around pegs as shown. *(Fig. 1)* Loop wire around bottom peg, then return

wire to top, wrapping figure eights around opposite pegs. *(Fig. 2)*
3. Lift wire from jig. Press design flat with

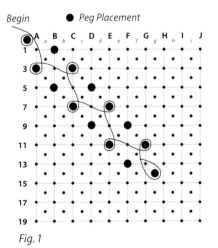

Fig. 1

nylon jaw pliers. Clip excess end wires.
4. Repeat steps 2 and 3 for second earring.
5. Attach a fish hook earwire in top loop of each figure eight wire designs.◖

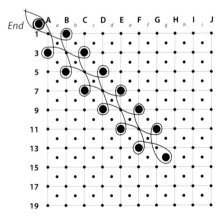

Fig. 2

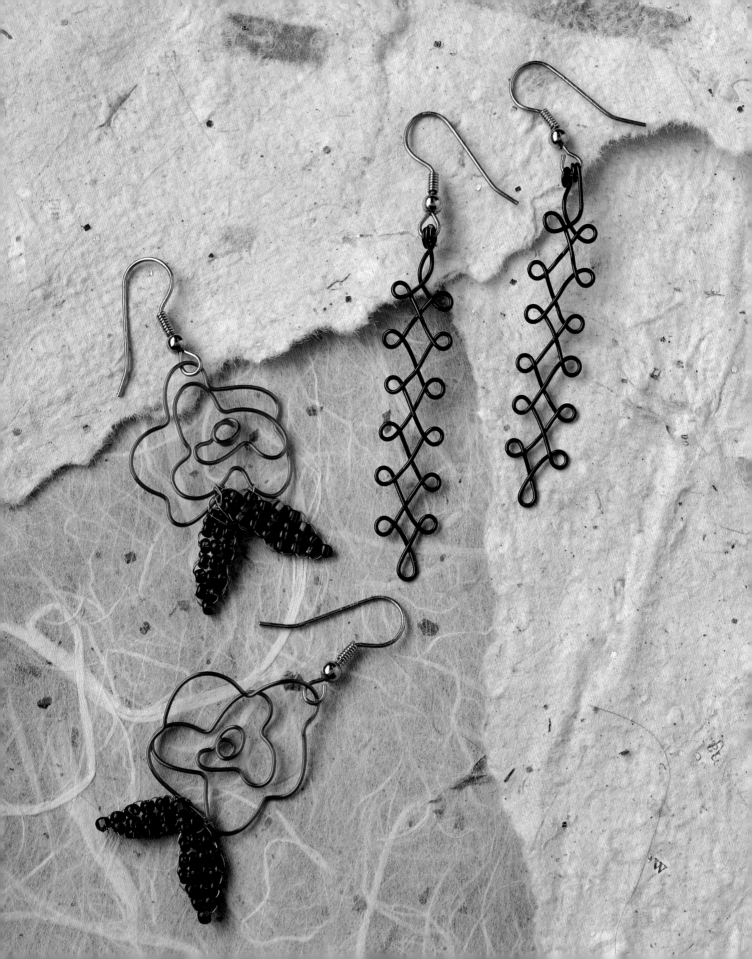

Shining Snowflake
Fashion Pin
(Pictured on page 103)

Designed by Diana Thomas

You Will Need

Supplies:
Silver beading wire, 24 gauge
Silver beading wire, 32 gauge
Crystal seed beads
Twelve crystal bicone beads
Seven silver beads, 8mm
Seven silver beads, 6mm
Six silver beads, 6mm
Three silver eyepins, 4"
Pin back
Jewelry glue

Tools:
Wire cutters
Round nose pliers

Follow These Steps

Make Arms of Snowflake:
1. Thread beads onto eyepin in this order:
   Seed bead
   4mm bead
   Seed bead
   Bicone bead
   Seed bead
   6mm bead
   Seed bead
   Bicone bead
   Seed bead
   8mm bead
   8 seed beads
   8mm bead
   Seed bead
   Bicone bead
   Seed bead
   6mm bead
   Seed bead
   Bicone bead
   Seed bead
   4mm bead
   Seed bead

2. Cut off any excess from eyepin, leaving 3/8" to form eye at end of wire with pliers. Form eye to secure beads.
3. Repeat steps 1 and 2 two more times.

Make Center of Snowflake:
1. Cut a 6" length of 24 gauge wire.
2. Crimp one end of wire and thread other end through a 6mm bead and 40 seed beads.
3. Cut off excess wire and crimp second end to hold beads in place.
4. Form a flat coil with beaded wire around the 6mm bead, hiding crimped ends underneath.

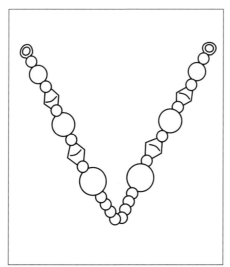
Fig. 1

Form Snowflake:
1. Bend each beaded eyepin into a "V" shape. *(Fig. 1)*
2. Cut an 18" length of 32 gauge wire to use as a tie wire.
3. Wrap tie wire around point of first "V" and use wire to join all three "Vs" together at points to form snowflake. *(Fig. 2)*

Assemble Pin:
1. Lay coil over center of snowflake and attach it to each arm of snowflake with tie wire.
2. Bring tie wire to center back of snowflake. Cut off excess wire and flatten to back with pliers.
3. Glue pin back to back of snowflake.◖

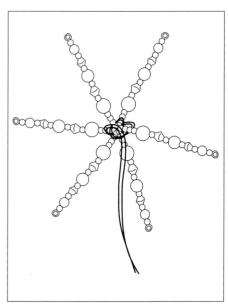
Fig. 2

Snow Crystal
Stickpin

Designed by Diana Thomas

You Will Need
Supplies:
Silver beading wire, 24 gauge
Package crystal seed beads
Silver bead, 2mm
Stickpin
Jewelry glue

Tools:
Wire cutters
Needlenose pliers

Follow These Steps
Form Leaves:
1. Cut a 36" length of 24 gauge wire. Crimp one end of wire.
2. To form first leaf, thread beads onto wire for 1-1/2". Push beads to a point 2" from crimped end. Loop beaded part of wire and twist two times to hold beads in place. *(Fig. 1)* Hold wires together 3/4" from leaf, and twist to form stem.
3. To form second leaf, thread beads onto wire for 1-1/2". Push beads to a point 1" from first leaf. Loop beaded part of wire and twist two times to hold beads in place. Hold wires together 1" from leaf and twist to form stem.
4. To form third leaf, thread beads onto wire for 1-1/2". Push beads to a point 3/4" from second leaf. Loop beaded part of wire and twist two times to hold beads in place.
5. Hold crimped end and wire at base of third leaf together 1/2" from leaf stem and twist to form stem before beginning flower.

Form Flower:
1. To form first petal of flower, string 2" of beads onto wire. Push beads to a point 3/8" from leaf stem. Loop beaded part of wire and twist two times to hold beads in place. Hold wires together 3/8" from petal and twist to form stem of petal.

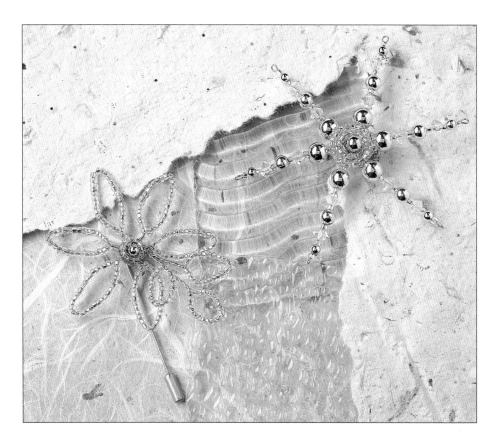

2. Working clockwise, repeat step 1 five more times.
3. Join first and sixth petals by wrapping wire around base of stem of first petal to form flower.

Flower Center & Stickpin:
1. Bring wire to topside at center of flower and thread the 2mm silver bead onto it. Wrap wire to back of flower, holding silver bead at center top.
2. Bring wire to front again and thread 12 seed beads onto wire. Twist to form loop.
3. Arrange loop over center bead and bring wire to back. Cut off excess wire and flatten end to back of flower with pliers.
4. Glue flower to stickpin.◖

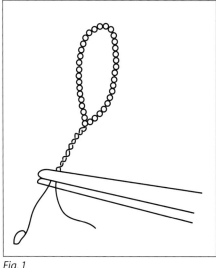

Fig. 1

Spiral Drops
Earrings
(Pictured on page 105)

Designed by Caren Carr

Finished Length of Earring: 2-3/4"

You Will Need
Supplies:
Aluminum wire, 17 gauge
Gold wire mesh
Two earring post backs, 5/8" diam.
Epoxy glue
Paper plates
Craft sticks

Tools:
Round nose pliers
Wire cutters
File
Scissors suitable for cutting gold mesh
Small binder clips

Follow These Steps
Prepare Earring Backs:
1. Cut two small 1" squares of gold wire mesh.
2. Adhere gold mesh to earring posts with epoxy cement. Use binder clips to keep it in place until dry. Check to see that epoxy has not come through the mesh to binder clip (lest binder be glued). Set aside.

Make Spirals (Flat Coils):
1. Cut two 7" lengths of wire and file the ends.
2. With round nose pliers, make tight flat coils, keeping 3/4" of wire straight. *(Fig. 1)* These are "post" spirals and should be large enough to cover the earring posts.
3. With round nose pliers, make a loop in the opposite direction on each. *(Fig. 2)*
4. Cut two 9" lengths of wire and file the ends.
5. With round nose pliers, make tight coils, keeping 3/4" of wire straight. These are the "drop" spirals.
6. With round nose pliers, make a loop in the opposite direction on each.

Assemble Earrings:
1. Cut two 1-1/2" lengths of wire for connectors. File the ends.
2. Establish the layout of the earrings. *(Fig. 3)* Make sure that all directions of spirals are symmetrical
3. Thread a connector through the loop of the post spiral and use round nose pliers to form it into a secure loop to attach it to post spiral. Thread the other end of this connector through the loop of a drop spiral. Use round nose pliers to make a secure loop, keeping the loops in the same plane.

Fig. 1

Fig. 2

4. Repeat step 10 for other earring. Check to make sure that earring lengths match. If they do not, start over with a new connector piece for second earring rather than try to use the previously bent one. Set aside.
5. Remove binder clips from posts backs. Use the scissors to trim the gold mesh to fit. File edges.
6. Glue post spirals to mesh-covered posts with epoxy, avoiding getting any epoxy in the center. Hold together with binder clips until epoxy cures completely.◖

Fig. 3

Pictured at right (clockwise from left):Spiral Drops Pin, instructions on page 106; Spiral Drops Earrings, instructions on page 104; Spiral Hoops With Coils Earrings, instructions on page 107

Spiral Drops
Fashion Pin
(Pictured on page 105)

Designed by Caren Carr

Finished Size of Pin: 2"w x 3"d

You Will Need
Supplies:
Aluminum wire, 17 gauge
Gold wire mesh
Pin back, 1-3/4" wide
Epoxy cement
Paper plates
Craft sticks

Tools:
Flat nose pliers
Round nose pliers
Wire cutters
File
Scissors suitable for cutting gold wire mesh
Small binder clips

Follow These Steps
Prepare Pin Back:
1. Cut a piece of gold wire mesh the width of pin back and a length that would go around pin back 3- 1/2 times.
2. Crimp in edges 1/8", using flat nose pliers.
3. Wrap around bar of pin back. Crimp in raw edge and glue down with epoxy. Use a medium size binder clip to hold in place.

Make the Spirals:
1. Cut six 6" lengths of wire. File the ends.
2. With round nose pliers, form each wire length into a tight spiral, leaving 1/2" straight. (Fig. 1) This is the general size, but they do not have to match exactly.
3. Use round nose pliers to make a loop in the opposite direction on each. (Fig. 2)

Assemble the Pin:
1. Cut a 2" length of wire. Cut two 1-3/4" lengths of wire.
2. Establish the layout of the pin: On your work surface, place three spirals in a row with loops downward and place three spirals below them with loops upward. Vary the direction of the spirals.
3. Thread the 2" wire through the loop of the center top spiral. Use round nose pliers to form the connector piece into a secure loop to attach it to top spiral. Thread the other end of the connector piece through the loop of the center bottom spiral, and use round nose pliers to make a secure loop. Make sure loops of connector piece are on the same plane and toward the back of the piece.
4. Use the two 1-3/4" connector pieces to attach the bottom left and right spirals to the upper left and right spirals, in the same manner.
5. Arrange top spirals on mesh-covered bar. Attach spirals to bar with epoxy, being careful to glue only the most solid portions of the spirals (avoiding the center). (Fig. 3) It will be easier to glue one spiral at a time. Use binder clips to hold each spiral in place while glue dries.❮

Fig. 1

Fig. 2

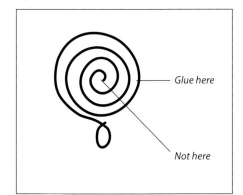

Glue here

Not here

Fig. 3

Spiral Hoops With Coils
Earrings
(Pictured on page 105)

Designed by Caren Carr

Finished Size of Earring (excluding finding): 2"

You Will Need

Supplies:
Aluminum wire, 17 gauge
Two French hook earring findings

Tools:
Round nose pliers
Wire cutters
File

Follow These Steps

1. Trace spiral shape in Fig. 1 and secure it to a flat work surface.
2. Cut a 12" length of aluminum wire. Cut a 6" length. File the ends.
3. With round nose pliers, coil the 6" wire like a spring. Inside should be large enough to accommodate two thicknesses of aluminum wire.
4. With round nose pliers, make a spiral with the end of one 12" wire, following the natural curve of the wire. Leave an 8" long tail.
5. Thread coil onto end of aluminum wire. *(Fig. 1)* Loop end of aluminum wire around in the same direction of its curve. and insert into other end of coil, until size of hoop in Fig. 1 is achieved.
6. Cut 3" off end of wire and file end. Using round nose pliers, make spiral in opposite direction.
7. Thread French hook earring finding onto this spiral. Tighten spiral to keep finding from slipping off.
8. Repeat all steps for second earring, making sure that finished earrings are symmetrical.❆

Fig. 1

Hammered Choker
Necklace
(Pictured on page 109)

Designed by Caren Carr

You Will Need
Supplies:
Aluminum wire, 17 gauge
Copper wire, 24 gauge
Small flat turquoise stone
Two 3" lengths silver chain (preferably featuring flat links—see photo of project)
Four silver jump rings
Silver hook and eye necklace clasp
Silver pendant hanger

Tools:
Round nose pliers
Wire cutters
File
Ballpeen hammer
Anvil, brick, or flat steel plate (old mattock head, old iron face, etc.)
Jewelry polishing cloth or silver polish

Follow These Steps
Choker:
1. Cut a 12" length of aluminum wire. File the ends. Spring the wire out to make a gentle curve.
2. With rounded end of the ballpeen hammer, working on your secure surface of an anvil, brick, or steel plate, hammer the wire as flat as possible. Adjust the curve of wire as you hammer; it will want to curve in on itself.
3. Polish.

Pendant:
1. Cut a 5" length of wire.
2. With round nose pliers, make an "S" spiral. *(Fig. 1)*
3. Hammer spiral as flat as possible.
4. Polish.
5. Fold the "S" around stone. Looking at the pendant from the side, you should see two parallel edges of hammered wire. *(Fig. 2)*
6. Cut a 15" length of copper wire and bend in half, with a gentle "U" at midpoint.
7. Holding stone and hammered wire together, loop the "U" of copper wire under two edges of the hammered wire. *(Fig. 3)*

8. Criss-cross the copper wire around the edges of the hammered wire, moving up around the stone. Lace as for shoes until stone is in place, being careful not to make bends in the copper wire.
9. Twist the two ends of the copper wire together for a distance of 3/8". Cut off excess.
10. With round nose pliers, make a loop in the same plane as face of pendant. Thread through pendant finding. Crimp securely. Wrap neck of loop with a small length of copper wire, if desired.

Assembly:
1. Thread choker piece through pendant finding.
2. Connect chain to hook and eye clasp with jump rings.
3. With round nose pliers, make loops toward the backside of the choker on each end. Connect chain to ends of choker with jump rings.◖

Fig. 1

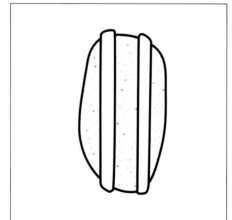

Fig. 2

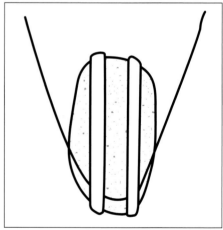

Fig. 3

Pictured (clockwise from center): Spiral Hoops Earrings, instructions on page 111; Hammered Choker Necklace, instructions on page 108; Hammered Spirals Earrings, instructions on page 110

Hammered Spirals
Earrings
Pictured on page 109

Designed by Caren Carr

You Will Need
Supplies:
Aluminum wire, 17 gauge
Two French hook earring findings

Tools:
Round nose pliers
Wire cutters
File
Ballpeen hammer
Anvil, brick, or flat steel plate (old mattock head, old iron face, etc.)
Jewelry polishing cloth or silver polish

Follow These Steps
1. Cut two 6" lengths aluminum wire and file the ends.
2. With round nose pliers, and working toward the natural curve of the wire, make a spiral with each piece of wire to match the shape in Fig. 1.
3. Establish the "right side" of each earring and lay them out on your table. *(Fig. 2)*
4. With the rounded end of the ballpeen hammer, working on your secure surface of an anvil, brick or steel plate, hammer a spiral, holding it by the 1-3/4" straight end of wire. This is your "handle." *(Fig. 1)* As you hammer, this "handle" will not remain in the same flat plane as the spiral and work surface. This is expected and you can hold the end of the wire up at a 30- degree to 40-degree angle. This will keep you from hammering yourself! As you hammer, the spiral will change in shape slightly. Therefore, hammer some on one earring spiral and then the other, comparing them often, until the desired texture is achieved. Make sure that you are hammering the "right side" of each.
5. Cut off the 1-3/4" handle of each earring.

With flat nose pliers or your fingers, bend remaining unhammered wire into the same flat plane as the earring spiral.
6. Use round nose pliers to bend end of wire into a gentle curve in the opposite direction. *(Fig. 3)* Compare earrings and cut off wire as needed to achieve matching shapes.
7. Thread through loop of French hook earring findings. Use round nose pliers to secure loops.
8. Polish.◖

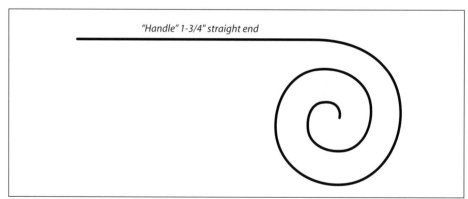

"Handle" 1-3/4" straight end

Fig. 1

Fig. 2

Fig. 3

Spiral Hoops
Earrings
(Pictured on page 109)

Designed by Caren Carr

Finished Size of Earring (excluding finding): 1-3/4"

You Will Need
Supplies:
Aluminum wire, 17 gauge
Two French hook earring findings

Tools:
Round nose pliers
Wire cutters
File

Fig. 1

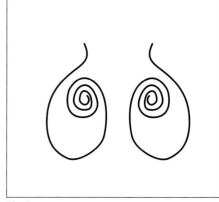

Fig. 2

Follow These Steps
1. Trace shape in Fig. 1 and secure it to a flat work surface.
2. Cut two 9" lengths of aluminum wire and file the ends.
3. With round nose pliers, form a tight spiral with end of one wire until spiral size in Fig.

1 is achieved. Hold the spiral in place on the pattern and curve remainder of wire around until hoop size is achieved. Cut off end of wire as needed, leaving 1/2" of wire.
4. Thread end of each wire through bottom loop of earring finding. With round nose

pliers, make a secure loop in the opposite direction.
5. Repeat steps 3 and 4 for second earring, making sure that finished earrings are symmetrical. (Fig. 2)◖

Double Stone Pendant
Necklace
(Pictured on page 113)

Designed by Caren Carr

Finished Length of Pendant: 3" from leather cord (dependent on size of stone)

You Will Need

Supplies:
Aluminum wire, 17 gauge
Silver beading wire, 24 gauge
Leather cord, one yard
Two polished semi-precious stones (shown are amethyst and citrine)
Two silver crimp end findings
Hook and eye clasp

Tools:
Flat nose pliers
round nose pliers
Wire cutters
File

Follow These Steps

1. Cut aluminum wire to the following three lengths: 3", 2-1/4", and 1-3/4"
2. Use flat nose pliers to make a "U" shape from the 3" wire. *(Fig. 1)*
3. Use round nose pliers to make loops at each end of the 2-1/4" and 1-3/4" lengths of wire. Make these loops facing each other, and large enough to accommodate aluminum wire. *(Fig. 2)* It is best if the loops are toward the natural curve of the wire.
4. Cut two 15" lengths of 24 gauge wire. Wrap each stone with enough wire to hold stone secure. Shake well to test. *(Fig. 3)*
5. Twist wire ends together at top of each stone for a distance of 3/8". Thread twist through loop at bottom of each straight piece of wire. Cut off excess wire and use round nose pliers to make a loop. *(Fig. 4)* Crimp securely.
6. String stone elements onto the "U" piece of wire.
7. With round nose pliers, make loops from the remaining straight ends of the right angled piece, parallel to each other and toward the back of the piece. *(Fig. 5)*
8. Cut a 12" length of 24 gauge wire. Wrap bottom of "U" with 24 gauge wire. This is a spacer, and can have some irregularities to it. Tuck under ends.
9. String leather cord through loops of "U" piece.
10. Adjust length. Finish ends with crimp end findings and hook and eye findings.◖

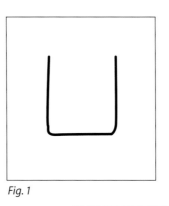

Fig. 1

Fig. 2

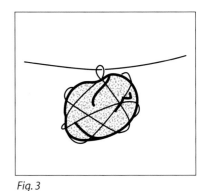

Fig. 3

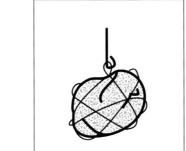

Fig. 4

Fig. 5

Pictured (clockwise from top right): Blue Beaded Dangles Earrings, instructions on page 115; Double Stone Pendant, instructions on page 112; Teardrops With Bronze Beads Earrings, instructions on page 114

Teardrops With Bronze Beads
Earrings
(Pictured on page 113)

Designed by Caren Carr

Finished Length of Earring (excluding earring finding): 2"

You Will Need
Supplies:
Aluminum wire, 17 gauge
Six bronze crow beads
Two French hoop earrings findings

Tools:
Round nose pliers
Wire cutters
File

Follow These Steps
1. Trace copy of shape in Fig. 1 and secure it to a flat work surface.
2. Cut two 12" lengths of aluminum wire and file the ends.
3. Thread one bronze crow bead onto one wire.
4. With bead at midpoint of wire, place wire on work surface with bead at bottom and the curve of wire upward (happy face). Cross your hands and pull the ends of the wire in opposite directions until the wire makes a loop the size of the loop on your tracing.
5. Place one end of wire through a crow bead and the other end through the same crow bead but from the opposite direction. (Fig. 2) In order to do this, you will momentarily lose the shape you just made. Pull wires gently through the bead, making sure that the bead stays in place at the top of the loop. Pull until the loop is the size in your tracing.

6. When wires have been pulled to desired shape and bead is in place, bend the two wire ends upward, then bend tightly at right angles across top of bead. (Fig. 3)
7. Twist wires together tightly three times. (Fig. 4)
8. Squeeze ends of wire together and slide crow bead down as far as possible, noting how much wire the bead covers.
9. Slide crow bead up, cut one of the wires so that the end will not protrude up out of the bead. Cut other wire just enough to

make a loop with round nose pliers.
10. Loop this wire through loop of French earring wire and tuck into top of bead. Make sure that loop is on perpendicular plane to earring.
11. Repeat steps 3-10 for other earring, checking shape against the first earring often.
12. With your fingers, squeeze each earring gently until earring is in desired teardrop shape.◖

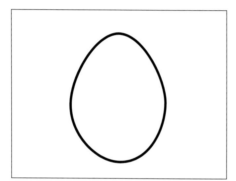

Fig. 1

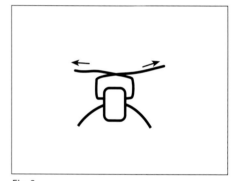

Fig. 3

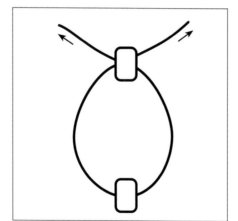

Fig. 2

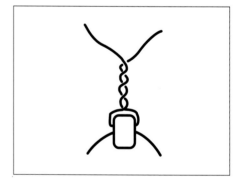

Fig. 4

Blue Beaded Dangles

Earrings

(Pictured on page 113)

Designed by Caren Carr

Finished Length of Earring (excluding earring finding): 1-3/4"

You Will Need

Supplies:

Aluminum wire, 17 gauge
Four blue crow beads
Two French hook earring findings

Tools:

Round nose pliers
Wire cutters
File

Follow These Steps

1. Trace copy of shape in Fig. 1 and secure it to a flat work surface.
2. Cut two 12" lengths of aluminum wire and file the ends.
3. With midpoint of one wire at Point A and the curve of wire facing down (sad face), cross your hands and pull the ends in opposite directions until the wire makes a loop the size of the loop on your tracing.
4. Place one end of wire through crow bead and the other end through same bead but from the opposite direction. *(Fig. 2)* In order to do this, you will momentarily lose the shape you just made. Pull wires gently through the bead, making sure that the bead stays in place at the top of the loop.
5. When wires have been pulled to desired shape, and bead is in place, bent the two ends of wire upward, then bend them tightly at right angles across top of bead. *(Fig. 3)*

6. Twist wire ends tightly three times. *(Fig. 4)*
7. Squeeze ends of wire together and slide crow bead down as far as possible, noting how much wire the bead covers. Slide crow bead back up. Cut one of the wires so that end will not protrude up out of bead. Cut the other wire just enough to make a loop with round nose pliers.
8. Loop this wire through loop of French earring wire and tuck into top of bead. Make sure that loop is on perpendicular plane to earring.
9. Repeat steps 3-8 for other earring, checking shape against the first earring often.◖

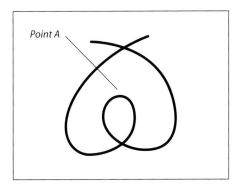

Fig. 1

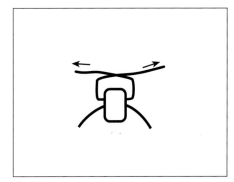

Fig. 3

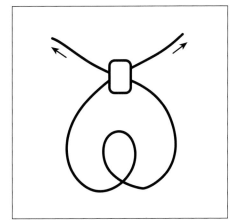

Fig. 2

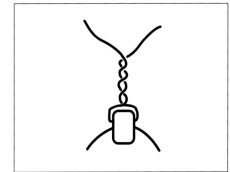

Fig. 4

Hairsticks with Red Dangles
Hair Ornament

Designed by Caren Carr

Finished Length of Hair Ornament: 10-1/4" (depending on length of chopsticks)

You Will Need
Supplies:
Red-covered copper wire, 16 gauge
Two chopsticks
Black spray enamel paint

Tools:
Round nose pliers
Wire cutters
File

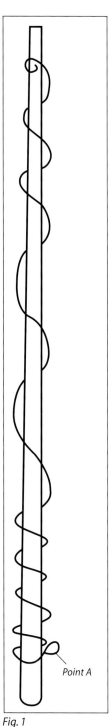

Fig. 1

Follow These Steps
Make the Sticks:
1. Spray-paint chopsticks black and let dry.
2. Cut two 18" lengths of wire. File the ends.
3. With round nose pliers, make a loop on one end of one wire.
4. Place loop at narrow end of chopstick and wrap chopstick, following Fig. 1. Cut off excess, if any, and file end.
5. With round nose pliers, make a loop at end (Point A in diagram), out from the chopstick and angled downward.
6 Repeat steps 3-5 for second stick.

Make the Dangles:
1. Cut two 5" lengths of wire and file the ends.
2. With round nose pliers, make a tight spiral with one wire, leaving enough wire to make an opposite "S" curve loop at top. *(Fig. 2)*
3. Repeat step 2 for second dangle.

Assemble Hairsticks:
1. Thread end of tight spiral through loop on top end of chopstick. Use round nose pliers to make a secure loop in opposite direction of spiral. Repeat on other hairstick.
2. Hold hairsticks up at angle used in hair. Adjust angle of hanging dangle loops, if needed.◖

Fig. 2

Black Wire Hoops

Earrings

(Pictured on page 119)

Designed by Caren Carr

Finished Length of Earring (excluding finding): 1-7/8"

You Will Need

Supplies:

Black coated copper wire, 16 gauge
Two French hook earring findings

Tools:

Round nose pliers
Wire cutters
File
Spice jar or other circular bottom with circumference to match Fig. 1 (if available)

Follow These Steps

1. Cut two 12" lengths of wire.
2. Trace circle pattern in Fig. 1. Place on work surface and, if available, place spice jar on circle.
3. Place the midpoint of the wire at Point A shown on pattern, with the curve of wire downward (sad face). Pull opposite ends until the wire makes the desired size circle. *(Fig. 2)*
4. Continue curving the wire around in a gently curve, being careful not to bend it, until the wires meet again at the top of the curve and the same size loop is made. *(Fig. 3)*

5. With ends of wire straight and at 180 degrees to each other, twist tightly a three-fourths turn. See top view—Fig. 4.
6. Cut off ends, leaving about 1/4" beyond loop. File the ends gently, without losing shape of twist.
7. Use round nose pliers to make a loop. *(Fig. 5)* Make other loop the same way, but first thread end through the bottom loop of a French earring finding.
8. Repeat steps 3-7 for other earring, checking hoop size often against the first earring. For second earring, attach earring finding in the opposite top loop so that earrings will be symmetrical. ❦

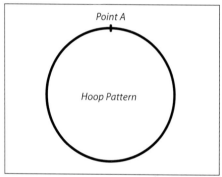

Fig. 1

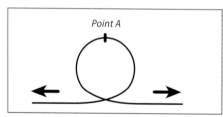

Fig. 2

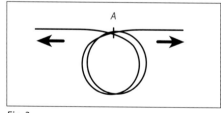

Fig. 3

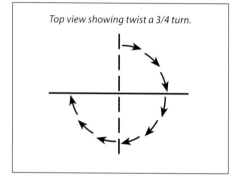

Fig. 4

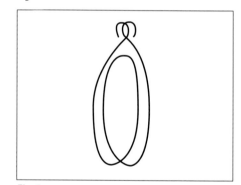

Fig. 5

Pictured (from top): Springy Choker Necklace, instructions on page 120; Black Wire Hoops Earrings, instructions on page 118

Springy Choker
Necklace
(Pictured on page 119)

Designed by Caren Carr

You Will Need
Supplies:
Covered colored copper wire, 16 gauge
(pkg. of 10 ft.)
Hook and eye clasp

Tools:
Round nose pliers
Wire cutters
Yardstick
File

Follow These Steps

1. Wrap entire length of wire from package around a yardstick, being careful to keep the same distance, if any, between wraps. TIP: This works best if you stand up, hold the yardstick parallel to the floor with roll of wire hanging down. Use gravity to create tension. Turn the yardstick into the wire rather than constantly manipulating the wire around the yardstick.

2. Carefully slide coiled wire off yardstick.

3. On ends of spring, establish where you will attach hook and eye clasp. Cut off wire, if needed. (Fig. 1)

4. Use round nose pliers to attach hook and eye clasp pieces to ends.

5. Adjust springiness evenly to fit your neck.

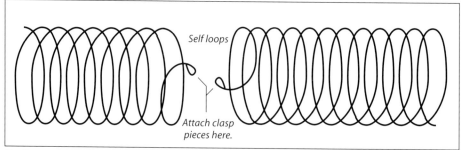

Fig. 1

Single Stone Pendant
Necklace
(Pictured on page 123)

Designed by Caren Carr

Finished Length of Pendant: 4" from leather cord (dependent on size of stone)

You Will Need
Supplies:
Aluminum wire, 17 gauge
Leather cord, 1 yd.
Polished semi-precious stone (shown is a chrysoprase)
Two silver crimp end findings
Hook and eye necklace clasp

Tools:
Flat nose pliers
Round nose pliers
Wire cutters
File

Follow These Steps
1. Cut a 3-1/2" length of aluminum wire and file the ends.
2. Gently bend wire in center around your thumb, making a "U." Set aside.
3. Cut a 15" length of aluminum wire.
4. Place midpoint of this wire on stone and wrap securely around stone three times as for a package. Keep wire ends straight and at 180 degrees to each other. (Figs. 1 and 2) Shake well to test security. If you have to start over, do so with a new piece of wire.
5. Keeping ends of wire at 180 degrees to each other, twist tightly for a distance of 2". (Fig. 2)
6. Cut off each end at 1/2" and file the ends.
7. Using round nose pliers, make two equal size loops, both in the same direction and large enough to accommodate aluminum wire.
8. Thread pendant onto "U" piece (made in step 2).
9. Use round nose pliers to make loops in ends of the "U" toward back of piece, parallel to each other, and large enough to accommodate leather cording. (Fig. 4)
10. String leather cord through loops of "U" piece.
11. Adjust length. Finish ends with crimp end findings and hook and eye clasp.⟪

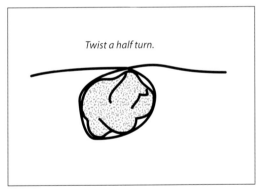

Twist a half turn.

Fig. 1

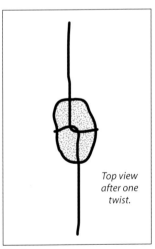

Top view after one twist.

Fig. 2

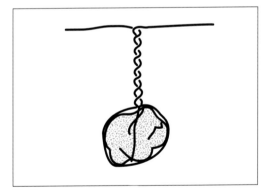

Fig. 3

Fig. 4

Wrist Ladder
Bracelet
(Pictured on page 123)

Designed by Pat McMahon

Finished Size of Bracelet: 1-1/4" wide

You Will Need
Supplies:
Copper wire, 12 gauge
Copper wire, 24 gauge
Silver solid core lead-free solder wire
24 silver pony beads
12 aluminum spacers, 1/2" long (from hardware store)
Jewelry glue

Tools:
Needlenose pliers
Wire cutters
File

Follow These Steps
1. Cut two 8" lengths of 12 gauge copper wire. Trim ends diagonally. File the ends smooth.
2. Using the template given, bend each wire into a circle. This is the diameter of the bracelet. Adjust template if you need to make the bracelet a larger or smaller diameter. Join the ends of each together with glue, overlapping the cut ends. *(Fig. 1)* Wrap the joint two or three times with 24 gauge wire to hold it in place. Trim ends away with wire cutters. Let glue dry thoroughly.
3. Unroll the silver solder wire and straighten it slightly. Working to your right and beginning with the wire outside one copper circle, leave the first 1-1/2" of silver wire free, then wrap the silver wire around the copper ten times, completely covering the joint. The wire will now be inside the circle.
4. Thread a silver pony bead, followed by an aluminum spacer and a second pony bead onto the silver wire. With the wire on the outside of the second copper circle, wrap over the joint ten times as before. *(Fig. 2)*
5. Repeat wrapping and stringing beads ten more times. Using the template, adjust the positions of the beads and wire so that spacing is even.

6. Refer to Fig. 3. Finish the wire wrapping by threading one pony bead and one aluminum spacer onto the end of silver wire you have been working with. Thread the last pony bead onto the 1-1/2" tail you left free at the start. Then thread that end up through the spacer and wrap it around the other wire between the first pony bead and the spacer. Pull it with pliers— gently, as solder is very soft and will break. When it has been wrapped once snugly, trim the end with the wire cutters. Use the pliers to flatten the end so it can be hidden between the beads. Repeat this procedure with the other wire end, wrapping it between the spacer and the last pony bead.◖

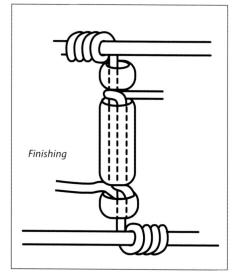

Finishing

Fig. 3

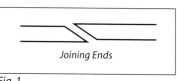

Joining Ends

Fig. 1

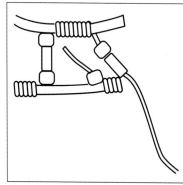

Fig. 2

Template

Pictured (clockwise from left): Single Stone Pendant, instructions on page 121; Tri-Color Twists Bracelet, instructions on page 124; Wrist Ladder Bracelet, instructions on page 122.

Tri-Color Twists
Bracelet
(Pictured on page 123)

Designed by Pat McMahon

You Will Need

Supplies:

Copper wire, 16 gauge

Green colored copper wire, 16 gauge

Gunmetal colored copper wire, 16 gauge

Two irregular shaped brass African beads, 1/2" diam. with large holes

Oval bronze African filigree bead, approx. 1" long with large hole

Jewelry glue

Tools:

Needlenose pliers

Round nose pliers

Wire cutters

File

Follow These Steps

1. Using one strand of each color copper wire, twist wires together. Follow directions in "Making a Perfectly Symmetrical Twist" in General Instructions. Make 21-1/2" of twisted wire.

2. Bend the twisted wire, following template, to conform to the shape in *Fig. 1*. The looped part of the bracelet will be the front with cut ends centered at back.

3. Loop one cut end through the loop formed in the front of the other side. *(Fig. 1)* Bring the cut end back to the back.

4. Thread one brass bead around to the back onto the continuous part of the wire. Repeat with the filigree bead and the remaining brass bead. *(Fig. 3)*

5. Holding one cut end with pliers, use the other pliers to unwrap 1/2" of the twist. Straighten the gunmetal piece. Trim the green piece off 1/2" from the cut edge. Wrap the copper end around both pieces of wire at 1/2". *(Fig. 2)*

6. Trim copper wire flush with twist. File any rough edges on the copper wire. File the gunmetal wire end to a flattened point. Repeat with the other cut end.

7. Thread one brass bead over the cut edge and push it up onto both layers of twist and out of the way. Repeat with the other bead on the other end. Center the filigree bead on the back of the continuous twist (single layer).

8. Push the straightened gunmetal end into the filigree bead and secure with glue. You may need to make space for the end by inserting the end of needlenose pliers into the space between the twist and the hole of the bead. If the end does not go in up to where the copper wire is wrapped, trim the end slightly, file it, and try again.

9. Slide the brass beads up to the filigree bead and force the two twists away from each other to hold them against the filigree bead. *(Fig. 4)*

10. Reshape wire as needed.◖

Fig. 1

Fig. 2 — finish off cut ends

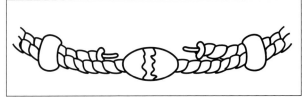
Fig. 3

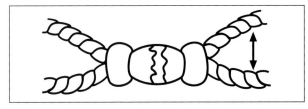
Fig. 4 — Force wires apart.

Template

Daisy, Daisy
Barrettes
Designed by Caren Carr

Finished Length of Barrette: 2-1/2"

You Will Need

Supplies:
Beading wire
Gold transparent rocaille beads
21 pink faceted plastic beads, 8mm
21 yellow faceted plastic beads, 8mm
Two barrette findings
Super glue or epoxy

Tools:
Optional: Tweezers for beadwork

Follow These Steps

1. Cut three lengths of beading wire: one 9" length and two 18" lengths.
2. Place together, aligning ends, and knot securely 3" from end.
3. String one rocaille bead onto length of wires.
4. Follow the Beading Diagram for beading the daisy. *(Fig. 1)* Note that barrettes have reversed colors. One has pink-yellow-pink flowers, the other has yellow-pink-yellow flowers.
5. After the third daisy of each barrette piece, place a seed bead, then knot securely.
6. Cut off ends so there is a 3" wire tail on each end.
7. Twist ends together neatly. Wrap ends through holes in barrette findings and loop each end up and around itself securely. Cut off excess and crimp ends securely.
8. Glue center beads onto to barrette findings. ❮

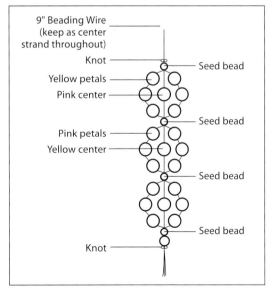

Fig. 1 — Beading Diagram

Metric Conversion Chart

Inches to Millimeters and Centimeters

Inches	MM	CM	Inches	MM	CM	Inches	MM	CM
1/8	3	.3	1	25	2.5	6	152	15.2
1/4	6	.6	1-1/4	32	3.2	7	178	17.8
3/8	10	1.0	1-1/2	38	3.8	8	203	20.3
1/2	13	1.3	1-3/4	44	4.4	9	229	22.9
5/8	16	1.6	2	51	5.1	10	254	25.4
3/4	19	1.9	3	76	7.6	11	279	27.9
7/8	22	2.2	4	102	10.2	12	305	30.5
			5	127	12.7			

Yards to Meters

Yards	Meters	Yards	Meters
1/8	.11	3	2.74
1/4	.23	4	3.66
3/8	.34	5	4.57
1/2	.46	6	5.49
5/8	.57	7	6.40
3/4	.69	8	7.32
7/8	.80	9	8.23
1	.91	10	9.14
2	1.83		

Index